Seven Nights

In

Morocco

Mark D K Berry

Copyright © 2022 - Mark DK Berry - www.MarkDKBerry.com

ISBN: 978-0-6485395-1-3 (eBook)
ISBN: 978-0-6485395-2-0 (Paperback)

No parts of this publication may be reproduced, stored in a retrieval system, or transmitted in any form or by any means, electronic, mechanical, photocopying, recording, or otherwise, without the prior written permission of the copyright owner.

This book is sold subject to the condition that it shall not, by way of trade or otherwise, be lent, resold, hired out, or otherwise circulated without the publisher's prior consent in any form of binding or cover other than that in which it is published and without a similar condition including this condition being imposed on the subsequent purchaser. Under no circumstances may any part of this book be photocopied for resale.

Some names and identifying details have been changed to protect the privacy of individuals.

Cover Photography & Artwork:
(Licence: Free for personal & commercial use: creativecommons.org/licenses/publicdomain/)
Morocan desert dunes adapted from - www.pikrepo.com/fbqia/morocco-cms-cc-by-brown-desert-during-daytime
Moroccan dune and night sky adapted from - www.piqsels.com/en/public-domain-photo-jtyzv

This Is Africa	1
The Grand Taxi	17
Just Keep Calm And Carry On	27
Tuareg	35
Kasbah	51
Animus Est Solvo	58
The Stars That Guide Us	71
The Persistent Breeze	79
Trekking Out	86
Setting Up Camp	94
In The Land Of The Silvery Blue	109
Why They Call It "Survival"	113
Hotel Palmerie	118
Une Bierre	130
Arabian Nights	142
By All The Gods	148
Movie Town	161
Travelling Through Time	174
Ships That Pass In Moroccan Nights	184
The High Adventures Of The Unknown	192

This Is Africa

I take the 140 bus from outside Harrow train station and arrive at Heathrow an hour later. It's 1:40 pm on Saturday 4th March 2006 and I'm at the start of a week-long solo adventure. I'm aiming to get to the Sahara desert in southern Morocco, but that's just a loose plan at this stage. Mostly, I intend to go with the flow and see where it takes me.

It turns out that Royal Air Maroc check-in is at Lufthansa, the baggage drop is at British Airways, and their flight bookings are at Air France. When I find the Air France check-in, I'm told by a South African who is waiting in the queue that he has been waiting there for one and a half hours. So I give up trying to book my internal Moroccan flight at Heathrow and head to the International check-in desk just as it opens.

It's the first time in my life that I have been at the front of an airport check-in queue. I bend down to lock up my rucksack and by the time I stand up again, twenty people have taken my place. But the processing happens quickly and I'm soon through. I realise I haven't put an address-tag on my ruck-sack, but it's gone already. A prayer goes out to it and I hope we will meet again. I head back to the desk at Air France but the queue hasn't moved, and so I go through security to the International departure lounge and look for something to eat.

Duty-free is a con and the food there is expensive. Terminal Two is small and there appear to be no fast-food options anywhere except for one, a sushi bar set-up in the middle of the court, but the prices start at fifteen pounds per dish. They have some sandwiches on offer, but it is mainly bread with barely any filling. I settle for an over-priced coffee and to write.

After travelling down the west coast of Spain two years ago carrying a ruck-sack, a large sleeping-bag, a tent, and a guitar, I'm pleased by how much lighter I have made my pack this time. I haven't brought the guitar along this time, as I have no intention of busking, but I have improved my equipment, making it much more suitable for travel, more compact and a lot lighter. The only obvious error in my kit choice so far has been my socks. They are *smart-wool*, whatever that means, but they feel clammy upon first wear. I also realise that it may have been a mistake not to wear in the new hiking trainers before leaving. I am dressed in light wick khaki hiking trousers with multiple pockets and zip-off legs, and I have a hiker's fleece top. Last time I looked like a vagrant, this time I look like a cliché travel-adventurer. But it's hard not to look like one, since the most suitable way to travel is to dress like one. Last time I journalled my trip, and that experience taught me a lot (available as *"The Road To El Palmar"*). This is my first solo trip since then, and I plan to journal about this one too. Since I feel better prepared this time, and I know more about what to expect, I intend to push the envelope further with a plan to wild-camp in the deserts of Morocco, if I can.

I still don't feel the holiday vibe. Maybe last night's emotional low is still lingering, which had me feeling anxious. I don't like the lead up, the wait to go, but once I am in motion, that usually lifts fairly quickly. There is a wild romance to be found in travel. It's the thrill of being anonymous. There is something sexy about that. A romantic allure smouldering beneath the surface on trips through strange places. I try to imagine that anything could happen here, but it's hard to believe of Heathrow Terminal Two. I have barely settled in to muse and write and it's already time to go to my gate.

I make it to Gate 10 only to be told that I should be at Gate 11, which is at the opposite end of the Terminal. It's an odd mistake for me to make, I usually double-check these things. I blame the coffee, and then head back the other way and thankfully am not too late. I prefer to do things with plenty of time to spare these days, especially with flights. Taking this approach then allows for the luxury of making the odd mistake while still allowing time to enjoy the journey without breaking into a sweat. Writing has helped in this endeavour. I savour the time stuck in a place where most people might prefer not to linger. I find it gives me time to jot down my thoughts while I watch people around me doing their thing. There is something about the travel-writing ritual that I love. It feels magical to let the pen flow across the page as it conjures adventure in real-time. I'm even more wilfully inviting the magic to embrace me on this trip and what better place to do that than in North Africa.

We are twenty minutes late taking off into a setting sun before banking to head south. The skies are clear and it looks like a mid-August day out there, but I know it isn't. A short while later, I see Portsmouth moving below us and a pang of nostalgia hits me as I recall the two years I spent living there. I was in love with a woman, living with her in a house on a quiet street in Southsea. It was a good time, despite it ending in yet another failed relationship, we never spoke again. I wonder about the carnage we leave behind us in our wake and a sigh escapes me. This trip has begun in nostalgic reverie, thinking about the best of times and the worst of times. I soon dismiss the moody feeling and turn my thoughts back towards the moment that I'm in and, of course, the adventure that awaits.

If I land at Casablanca slightly later than scheduled, it will add a challenge to my plan of getting an internal flight tonight to Ouarzazate (pronounced *Wazzazat*). I still don't feel in much of a holiday mood and wonder if I've outgrown such things. That would be a shame. I idly watch the in-flight map as we move across it. Africa isn't that far away from England in the grand scheme of things. I consider how cultures seem to differ more across the distance of Latitude than Longitude, and I wonder if that's because of the sun and climate difference. I look at my brand new, super-fly, high-tech watch - another ridiculous purchase that makes me look like a travel geek - it says we are at 1670 meters above sea level. The digital compass on it appears to be correct to the plane map, so maybe the plane and cabin-pressure don't affect it as I thought they might. I wonder how the contraption works and whether the height it shows is accurate. The monitor screen says we are at 37,000 feet, but I don't know the metric conversion [Edit: 11,277 metres, so the watch was incorrect or I read it wrong].

I'm feeling strangely detached, and this surprises me. When flying to Spain I was ecstatic, while this time I feel numb. Back then I was full of eager wit and prose, annoyingly so, but now I have nothing, absolutely *nada* to write about. It doesn't bother me too much, but this isn't what I expected.

Aha! The measurements on the screen have just changed and tell me we are 1300 meters above sea level, so my watch seems to be about 300 meters out [and the rest]. Maybe it's referring to ground level, not sea level... Jesus! When did I become this much of a goddamn nerd?

We land twenty minutes late at Mohammed International V, Casablanca. The airport is pleasantly quiet. I make a mental note to ask for a front seat in the future. I did okay with my booking and got to enjoy the roomy middle window seat beside the emergency exits, but this meant I had further to go to get out. Luckily, the plane was going on to Marrakesh, so half of the passengers stayed on board and didn't delay me from exiting.

I met an Australian couple on the flight when I took a wander up the aisle, and they seemed to think I would like it in their country. We got talking about that, but then I forgot to ask them where they were going in Morocco or if they had any suggestions. Too late now.

I finally get through passport control, and my bag is waiting for me doing circuits on the carousel. It would have happened quicker, except I got sent back the first time. I had gone looking for the internal flight desk - that I didn't find - then got redirected back the other way by a belligerent guard. I then go out of the wrong passport control exit and appear to be at a main-desk outside. It confuses me to find myself there. I'm sure it wasn't supposed to happen this way. A lady at the desk sees me dithering and welcomes me to Morocco. After asking me how she can help, I tell I her need a flight to Ouarzazate. She deftly organises one for me on the spot. Before finalising it, she looks up at me. I am fidgeting around, wanting her to hurry up. Reading me correctly, she tells me to relax and stop my panicking, but she does it in such a way that I can't get annoyed and just melt. There is something about her smile, her confidence, and her ease that calms me. She is right, of course, I am on holiday, so what am I thinking getting all stressed? It's time to enjoy myself and relax.

I have to say Arabian women are stunning, with a dark and sultry look in their eye that is very attractive. She disarmed my sketchy mood with it in an instant. She was aware of the effect she had on me. I've spotted a few women here with a similar Persian look, and I'm strangely smitten by them.

The next leg of my flight costs me fifteen hundred dirham, also known as MAD, amusingly. I figure out with a rough calculation that equates to about one hundred English pounds sterling, but then I remember my maths is not *that* good. Unfortunately, my Visa card doesn't work in her machine, which is a worry, and I head over to an exchange kiosk where I change up the four hundred Euro I brought with me, ready for such eventualities. They convert my Euro into MAD money and I get about four thousand dirham in return, but I can't figure out if that is good or not for GBP. I am too tired to think, and so I just take it and go back and pay the lady for the open-ended ticket to Ouarzazate.

She tells me that the flight will return at six am any morning and there is one flight per day, I just have to turn up. I thank her and then go to the internal check-in desk. It's closed. Uncertain what to do, I try the next one along for the hell of it, and they seem happy to help. They take my rucksack without asking to see my passport. Strangely, my bag weighs in at seven-point-two kilos, while back in the UK it had been only six-point-nine. Had somebody added something? I couldn't see why someone would, and so decide not to mention it. I then go looking to buy water and, while trying to purchase it, use Spanish lingo instead of French, and we end up a bit confused. Me not knowing either language much past *"hello"* or *"thank-you"* doesn't help. The water is eight dirham, which they then count out for me. I look at the change, wondering how I will ever get my head around the conversions. It thought one dirham equated to six pence, but that doesn't seem right either. There should be a trick to currency conversion, but damned if I know it.

I find my connecting plane and board. We then sit on the runway for an annoyingly long time. I don't yet know where I will stay in Ouarzazate and it will probably be after one in the morning when I get there. I am curiously relaxed about it all now, thanks in part to the lovely smile of the lady back at the check-in desk. There is something soothing about Moroccans, they seem chilled out. The weather is warm, a t-shirt would have done, and my watch says it is twenty-eight degrees. Getting back to exchange-rate maths, I ponder it further, eventually concluding that one pound is worth fifteen dirham, but also accepting I may still be wrong about that [During the edit of this book I looked it up and on 4th March 2006, 100 MAD = 6.26 GBP]. I pull out my notebook to write and to dispel the annoyance of being stuck on the tarmac.

When coming in to land at Casablanca, the city had looked like a golden spider's web from above and now drizzle hits the window of the plane making more curious patterns with the light. I am feeling a little deflated by the wait, and I can't understand the English interpretation we're receiving on the reasons for it. The plane is empty, and I have a row to myself.

It's a decent sized Boeing, thank god. I was half expecting some bi-plane affair for the internal flight over Africa.

I realise that I'm less nervous about arriving in a small town like Ouarzazate than I would be if it were a big city. Cities are cold and anonymous places and that can make them dangerous. Small towns offer a slower pace, a friendlier smile, and a less militant rule, or so I think. People help strangers in small towns. I have the feeling that if I arrive at an even more stupid hour than I hope to, somehow I will get by in Ouarzazate. Not sure why I feel this way and, as I consider it, logical thinking prevails and I dig out my *Lonely Planet Guide Book*, to find a few hotels and note them down. I should be able to get a cab at the airport and maybe some advice on a safe hotel from a taxi driver. Then, hopefully, bed down for the night before moving on tomorrow heading further south into Morocco.

I enjoy functioning in this way - nothing planned, just flow and decide as I go. I got the hang of it in Spain, eventually, and it made me realise just how stiff and scheduled my life had become. This trip I'm deliberately seeking to avoid pre-planning anything much beyond basic safety. I have a hunch Africa will encourage me in this more fated approach to decision making, and so far, so good.

Making this flight tonight means that there's a good chance of reaching the Sahara, as I had hoped. This means I might get some time to do a spot of wild-camping in the rocky wilds I read about outside of the towns after that.

I still don't feel the holiday buzz, despite being fully immersed in the adventure now, and I find that odd. But I am looking forward to the solitude of the desert, and glad of the decision to bypass the big cities along the way. I long to be in a place with fewer rules, fewer people, less demand, less human influence, and somewhere more tuned in to nature. I need to feel a sense of freedom again, and I hope to find that in the unfamiliar place that I am bound.

The night sky is clearing, and only thirty minutes later, we take off. Then there he is - Orion, one of my favourite star groups. It's the first constellation that I spot as I peek out of the plane window into the darkness after take-off. He has been a familiar companion on all my travels. I have spotted him in the Northern and the Southern Hemispheres and on most all the trips I've ever taken. He often jumps out at me when I look into the night skies.

We are flying high over the African continent now. Pockets of golden city light flicker below us with a half-crescent moon hanging above. Everything in between is a blanket of pitch-black darkness without edges, and it appears soft to me, like velvet. The moment transports me back to a night camped on the empty beach between El Palmar and Conil in west Spain. It was the location of the Battle of Trafalgar, as it had drifted north from the marker that named the battle. Looking out of my tent that night at the crescent moon hanging over the sea, I had thoughts of Arabia on my mind for reasons that I couldn't fathom at the time. It held me spellbound then, and was a magical night. I later thought about Morocco and if it might be a future destination. I was headed to Tarifa the next day, and once there, I briefly laid eyes on the North coast of Africa before turning around and making my return journey back to London. My hunch had been right, two years on, and here I am. This trip has been a long time coming.

Unfortunately, my life in England slowly came undone after that trip. It seemed to get harder for a long time, though maybe that's an age thing too - I will be forty later this year, and I am finding it to be a confusing age. Not long after returning from Spain, I split up with the woman I was living with. We'd been together for seven years, so it was a big change. I moved out of our house in South Harrow and spent the next few months living in a purple truck on the streets of London. That was ridiculous, in retrospect, and I think I went mad for a while. Grief does that. Though it *was* an interesting way to pass the time, and in the end it made for a healthy challenge and gave me something to take my mind of things. That winter, once I had finally stopped feeling heartbroken and sorry for myself, I took a little room near my workplace in Harrow on the Hill. I planned to save money while I tried to figure out what to do with the rest of my life. The experience of hitting forty was scaring me. For a while I thought I might move to El Palmar and join the people I'd met there and jump in on their surf vibe, but the idea soon waned, and it no longer felt real to me. I made no further plans after that, because I didn't really know what to do. I was hoping this trip might serve as an inspiration to help me figure it all out. One thought that has become gradually more clear to me is that I'm not sure England is my home anymore. I was born there, but I've moved around so much that sometimes I feel like I don't belong there. I always had the feeling that I would leave England one day.

And so now here I am, flying over the continent where humanity may have had its origins. My aim is to reach the Sahara desert. An idea arrived at by sticking a pin in a map and thinking it looked like an adventurous place to go. Since I'd seen North Africa from Tarifa, and it had appealed back then, I just thought why the hell not? Just do it! So I did.

It's a long time since I visited in Africa, but she's a continent I always felt drawn to return to. She has a way of affecting you, getting into your bones, making you long for her, and that longing will continue for the rest of my life. I was ten years old the last time I set foot here, and I came a few times before that. Not here in the north, but much further south to Zimbabwe - Rhodesia at the time - where I had family living. Those trips as a child gave me vibrant, colourful, and rich memories. As alive in me now as they were when I engaged in them. Memories can feel like a bond, a relationship made to a person, a place, a time, or to the land itself. Something in me bonded with Africa and I've wanted to come back ever since.

I feel my ears changing pressure and am distracted from reminiscing as we begin our descent towards Ouarzazate where this adventure will begin. I must remember to offer a blessing when I leave the airport. I'll do it by making a small honour and prayer to the country, to the land, and to the journey before me as I take my first steps here. Two men taught me ways of dealing with the spiritual aspects of our journey through life and I want to mention them because they hold such amazing knowledge; Malidoma Patrice Somé and Martín Prechtel. Elders from Africa and Guatamala respectively. I sought them both out a year or so ago, and they taught me about shrine work, about dealing with our grief using ritual and honour, and about the value of talking to our ancestors, as well as ways to show respect to the spirits of an unfamiliar place. Hopefully, if I do it right, the spirits here will let me pass through their home without a fuss. And with a bit of luck, they'll steer me on towards good things. If I don't honour them, then who can say what trouble I might get into. This is Africa, and it's best to greet her on her terms. She still carries an indigenous heartbeat.

We circle over Ouarzazate from a distance. I see two bright stars above it and they look like the eyes of a snake. This continent is where I first fell in love with snakes. Smart - my Gran's gardener in Bulawayo - took me into the garden and showed me two poisonous ones he'd caught there. They fascinated me from the moment I saw them. Those stars sparkle now, like snake's eyes, watching me. They shift and change as I gaze at them until they look like the posts of a gate and I fancy them to be the gateway to Africa.

The land has kept its secrets hidden from me by my arriving at night, and I can't see much as we make the final descent onto the runway. I won't know what kind of terrain I'm in until dawn light tomorrow. It looks to be flat all around, but beyond the edges of the airport fence there isn't much that being giving away and it is shrouded in darkness.

My bag is first out onto the carousel. No passport checks here, and I like that. Airport casual. I wander out into the warm night air and stop outside the main doors to light a cigarette. A small bat flies around in the orange street-lights of the car park. It's a dry place I've arrived in and dusty too, but it's windless. A lone cop stands watching me from a few feet away. I greet him and he gives me a silent nod in return. Nothing gives me cause for concern here; no weirdness, no crazy baying locals, no hassle so far. I wasn't sure what I would find, and this is a promising start. Some locals stand a little further off, but they're not paying me any attention either. I wonder about protection, not that I feel threatened at all, but just because it's something to consider when travelling alone in foreign places. I've packed a large hunting knife in my ruck-sack and was half expecting it to cause problems through customs, but it's come through without incident. It's wrapped and packed deep in my luggage to ensure they wouldn't consider it an accessible weapon. I have legitimate reasons for bringing it, as I plan to camp out in the wild.

It's ten minutes past midnight as I blow puffs of smoke

into the air and watch it linger above my head in the orange glow of the black night. I consider that the locals standing around in the car park are probably taxi drivers, so I wander over to find out and I'm right. I finish my smoke and then book one to take me to Hotel Baba.

He says fifteen dirham when I book it, but when I arrive he insists he said fifty. Stupidly, I had pulled out over a thousand dirham in a wad of notes I hadn't yet organised. I was too tired to argue, more concerned that Hotel Baba looked shut. Driving the short distance from the airport, the town appeared deserted, and it looked more like Baghdad after a year of bombing than Africa. It was dusty shoe-boxes for houses and hardly any light on anywhere in the streets or otherwise.

I pay him his fifty and then ask him to wait for a moment. Getting out, I push on the steel door that has Hotel Baba painted above it and it opens, and so I wave to the driver to let him know I won't need him further. Inside it looks like a dive, but I really don't care. The door peels back heavily, and steep concrete stairs lead up to where I am met at the top by the manager. He speaks pidgin English but is friendly enough. He then shows me to the only room they have left. It's a three-bedder for the price of a single, which is eighty-five dirham. At that price, I wonder if the cab driver stung me, but no matter, it's still a lot cheaper than London. The first ones always get you. It's the price you pay for knowledge when you travel and something to expect, nothing to feel ashamed of. You pay to learn the way.

The ambient light in the hotel is from fluorescent tubes and has a hint of yellow and green, maybe from the colour of the walls. It gives it a low-level flickering, almost clinical glow that makes me feel like I could be in a movie about Mexican gun-runners. It's kind of cool. I wonder what the hotelier thinks I am doing there. It's hardly the busiest place, and I don't expect to see many other foreigners. The air is dry and my throat feels rough from the dust already.

I look around my room, then put my shoes on the bed next to me so that the cockroaches will have to put effort in to reach them. I then roll out the funky new light-weight sleeping bag, ready to give it its first test run. I'm looking forward to that. The bed doesn't look the cleanest, but it doesn't look too scabious either. Over-all the room is okay. There are no windows, but I'm just glad to be somewhere that feels safe.

I didn't have time to do my ritual at the airport and there were people around, so I lay out some of the small trinkets I've brought with me. They are symbols and sentimental items that have meaning relevant to me and live on my shrine at home. I have brought ones that can travel easily. The reason I do this is that it helps connect me to the journey, not just travelling through Morocco, but through life. Doing this brings with it a sense of reverence to the act. It doesn't need much, just a few thoughts, some quiet words, a bit of respect for whatever is out there and might guide me. I express my feelings and emotions quietly. Whispering them gently into the unknown, speaking to whatever may be out there, and to the adventure that I am now on, and, of course, briefly talking to my ancestors. This doesn't take long. This is the stuff that Malidoma and Martin taught me. Such ritual behaviour may seem alien to our culture and it has taken nearly two years to feel comfortable doing it. I think that when we find ourselves alone in a world, in a place we aren't familiar with, that we come to understand the importance of talking to the gods, to the spirits, and to our ancestors. Maybe we want to feel less alone on the journey, and maybe they don't exist beyond our own imaginations. I felt shame at first, but soon realised its value with practice. And if it brings me a sense of comfort and strength at those times, then it works. The act of prayer is the oldest act known to man, and that must count for something in an age when gods have been replaced by businesses, machines, and modernity. When you travel off the beaten path alone, you need something to travel with you. I've been doing these kinds of libations for a few years now. It's been a deliberate attempt on my part to rekindle the pagan soul. Invading monotheistic organised religions stamped it out of my lineage when they swept through Britain thousands of years ago. I've been waking it back up. Engaging in this kind of practice almost daily since I learned to do it. Now I am certain that things have been improving in my life since I began it. The first attempts at doing it full-time came when I moved into the purple truck. It was to counteract the madness I was falling into, though maybe I did it to engage in the madness. Hard to be certain which, and probably depends on whom you ask. But I have been at it long enough now. It has become familiar for me to talk to my ancestors on nights like these. I no longer feel stupid for doing it. Alone, miles from anywhere, solitary and lost in space. By far the best time to connect with the unknown, and to our innate sense of the spiritual. In doing that, I now find my strength. Indigenous people understand this, and modernity has forgotten it. That's why I went to Malidoma Somé and Martin Prechtel to ask them to teach me how to reconnect with that. It helped me to put my life in the bigger picture, to reframe my sense of purpose. It worked, but I still have a way to go. If I hadn't started the conversation with my ancestors, then I would have remained disconnected from everything. And maybe that, in part, now draws me to put my feet on African soil again. I finish up and then put the items away, and then go to find the manager to speak to him about getting something to drink.

The Hotel Baba manager gets me a bottle of water and a cup of coffee from the closed café downstairs. I follow him down to have a look around, the place is quiet and empty. I'm liking that I feel a million miles away from the suburban concrete jungles of London. I head back upstairs. It's time to get some kip, to replenish and to get ready for tomorrow. I check my shoes and bag for scorpions, get in the habit of it, though I don't expect there to be any in this room. A guy on the plane had a cockroach in his dinner, and when he complained to the air hostess about it, she moved him to first-class with promises of free stuff. I saw him plant it there from a matchbox he carried with him in his shirt top-pocket. I think about that now and laugh. Then I lie down on the bed, shut my eyes, and within moments, I'm fast asleep.

The Grand Taxi

I'm up at 5:43 am and out with the dawn at 6:30 am. I feel fully rested. It always seems like I need less sleep when I'm on the move through unfamiliar places. The wind is blowing hard from the north and it's cold. Conveniently, the bus garage is right opposite Hotel Baba.

Some people sleep in makeshift tents outside on a large square of dusty, derelict land. I notice the remnants of small campfires in the streets. The bus station is busy already, and a man shouts destinations from within. I speak to him, and though his English is minimal, he seems to think my bus leaves for M'Hamid in an hour. He then points to an empty window booth, which I assume to be the place I can get a ticket.

According to my guidebook, M'Hamid is the southernmost point that I can get to and is the entry point for the Sahara desert. I find a shop and buy two bananas. The sky is clear and I can see mountain peaks, snow-capped and tall, covering the north-west line of the horizon far beyond the town. The sun doesn't break over the pink box-shaped adobe buildings until after 7 am and by then the town seems thoroughly awake. Cars and motorbikes rattle by with broken exhaust pipes in need of a service. I find another shop inside the station to stock up on cigarettes. I'm pleased to see a poster of the England squad in the shop, not because I like football, but because it's my first connection to home. Somehow England seems more appealing when I'm not there. It's amazing how quickly strange looks from strange people can make you miss being ignored by your fellow countrymen. So far I have had no real hassle here, but as always, the lowlifes want to talk to me and are drawn, almost magnetically, to seek me out. Their play is to gain something, and the approach is obvious when it begins, but a simple dismissal seems enough to bring no further attention from the ones around here.

I'm glad I've avoided Casablanca and Marrakesh. The bustle and chaos of big cities would have made me more reactive and that might have created trouble. At least I can acclimatise in these easier-to-manage surroundings. I wonder if this cold and blustery wind will warm up as the sun goes to work on the day. I can't see much past the buildings, so can't get an idea of the landscape around here other than the tips of those distant mountains. The town itself is dusty and devoid of anything green, except for the odd stump of what might have been a palm tree once. Talking of palm trees, in my rucksack is a Hennessey hammock that I plan to use tied between palm trees that I hope to find in the deserts outside of the towns. And now, it's time to go in search of a cup of tea to warm my body up from this morning chill.

The Grand Taxi that I take - when I discover the bus may not come until 2 pm - is the tattiest of the ones stood waiting outside the bus station. It doesn't get going until they fill it with six souls bound for Zagora. It seems Zagora is my best bet. I have been told it's most of the way to M'Hamid and is the last major town on the road in that direction. We eventually leave at 9 am with no sign of a bus for M'Hamid arriving soon, and we have two false starts before we get going.

The first false start occurs when a couple that were planning to come, don't. The woman suddenly got sick, vomiting on the ground outside the car, and then they left. So we all got back out again and sat around waiting for new travellers to come and fill their places. Finally, our driver finds someone and calls for us all to get in. It turns out to be a guy who has been following me around like a lost lamb and he tries to get in on my fare. I am unaware of the ruse until the driver asks me to pay for him, but my look of confusion uncovers his sneak attempt. They throw him out, along with a bit of cuffing from the driver for wasting everyone's time. We are back to waiting for at least one more paying passenger to show up.

My shadow then hung a little way off. I was hiding behind the car, but he maintained his gaze with an unblinking, almost loving look in his eyes. He didn't bother me all that much, other than just being odd and following me around. I'd felt there was a sadness about him. He was one of the lost souls of the world and it seemed like there was nothing left inside him, just a curious and glassy creepiness remained. I'd tried to be polite to him until I realised he was not going away. He latched onto me after floating over to engage and then ignored my attempts to shoo him off. I couldn't understand his language, and he couldn't understand mine. I soon realised he was freaky. It shone out of his mannerisms, and to be honest, he gave me the jitters. But even the lowliest souls I am finding easy to deal with so far. It would have been a lot more hectic in the cities, with a larger number of them to fend off, no doubt. This event is making me commended myself again on the decision to avoid the cities when choosing my arrival point.

Eventually, others show up to fill the gaps and our Grand Taxi leaves with a couple more women in the seats and some dogs in the boot. I am in the middle-back, with a large and well-dressed gentleman to my left and a larger lady to my right. We even have a motorbike lashed onto the roof. A curious moment transpires when the lady to my right argues loudly against having to get in next to me. Then she says something rough sounding, pointing at me as she does so, and everyone laughs. Seems I am the butt of some local racist joke. I can't understand a word of it, and rather than being annoyed or shamed, I find the episode to be culturally fascinating. Out here, I am a lower class of being, not revered or put up on a pedestal. I am somewhere down the bottom, possibly with the dogs, and I am lucky not to be in the boot and them in the middle-seat. I must have some standing with the driver. But if the lady's reaction is anything to go by, I'm a leper. Though I note her joke isn't good enough to change the seating arrangements. She is not happy about that. I smile at her and nod understandingly as she reluctantly squeezes her fat ass into the seat next to mine. She has done her utmost to avoid looking at me, and it remains that way for the entire journey. She really is that annoyed. Staring out the window and huffing whenever she has to acknowledge my presence. It has been interesting to observe, and I resist the desire to annoy her further.

As soon as we leave Ouarzazate, I realise I have landed on another planet. It is mile after mile of broken rocks and nothing much else. In the distance are those gorgeous High Atlas mountains. With their snowy peaks, they stand like sentinels on the horizon. A magnificent contrast against the endless flat landscape that surrounds us in all directions. The dry desert rock makes them look even cooler and more inviting. But I have my mission set; I am going south to the sands of the Sahara.

We drive for an hour and there is nothing much to see other than goat herders and the occasional glimpse of a waterless riverbed. Then there appear small and inexplicable explosions of random green. Sudden clusters of palm trees with grass around them. I can't understand how they are surviving out here in the desert. There is no sign of a river or a house for miles and yet sporadic clumps of vegetation exist. They can't qualify as oases, just small green manicured areas that spring up and then disappear no sooner than we see them. We just keep sailing on through it all relentlessly.

Another half-hour goes by much the same, and then we pass a river with water in it. That's exciting. I take it to be the river Draa with its source in those wonderful mountains and making its thousand kilometre run to the ocean. The river looks shallow, about thirty or forty feet wide, and it makes my journey-dulled senses leap to see it. I struggle to monitor it, but we turn a sudden and sharp bend and climb further on up into rocky hills. After that, I don't see the river again.

We arrive in the town of Agdz. A stall market is opening there and many cloaked and hooded figures are milling about. Some sit watching the world go by, while others sit and stare at their feet. There seems to be a lot of sitting around going on in Agdz, which I guess is not surprising if you live somewhere that looks like the moon and there's not much to do. The fashion of the day is to dress like an extra from a Star Wars movie, and it is an eerie sight. Dozens of people wearing dark-coloured cloaks that reach down to the ground and cover their entire body. All have large, pointy hoods that give them the appearance of being Obi-Wan Kenobi. It thrills me to think we can get out and investigate the market, but we don't stop in Agdz, just tear on through and I am disappointed. As we leave, the scenery changes, but only slightly. I can't grasp quite how, but everything seems more attractive after Agdz. It's still hard rock with some occasional random green bits, and then at some point the river comes into view again, and this time more frequently.

Another hour later, having passed through more small villages, we enter a long, flat expanse with a wide growth of palm trees to our left. The land is level here, maybe for farming. In the far distance, beyond the trees and spread out against the backdrop like a huge surrounding wall, is a long line of flat-topped mountains. It isn't the High Atlas this time, but another range, not as grandiose as the High Atlas mountains, and not tall enough to have snow-capped peaks, either. These remind me of the Grand Canyon in Arizona. I can make out flat, even-coloured layers distributed throughout the rock in grades. The stretch of road that we are now on, I assess to be the final run toward Zagora. I hope it is, as I can barely move and am tired of the journey and the constant disdain of my unfriendly female neighbour. The road is now lined with adverts for hotels and riverside campsites. I am looking beyond them for suitable places to wild camp, and notice most of the areas beyond the town have people working the land on farming plots with small earthen wall structures dividing them. I'm not sure that I will find solitude or suitable camp spots at the edge of town, but maybe by walking further out into the more distant flat expanse of the rocky desert, I might. Seeing that landscape, I can now put my fear of panthers and jackals to rest. Though they did once have lions in Morocco and could even lay claim to the largest of the big cats known as the Barbary lion. The last of those mighty beasts died in a zoo in New York in the 1960s and the last of the wild ones in the 1920s. It's long enough ago that lions are not on my danger-list when camping out here. From Ouarzazate all the way south there has been nothing but rock, it is a desert with very little sand, and I am not sure much can live in that, apart from the occasional basking lizard, maybe. Looking at that rocky desert beyond the farming divides, I expect my wildlife encounters will range somewhere between raggedy humans, biting camels, and maybe a few rogue dogs.

It has surprised me to see French-plated RV Campers, and they, more than any other vehicle, have been passing us by on the road. Their white, super-shiny exteriors make them seem invasive and out of place in this ancient rocky desert vastness. I look inside the vehicles as we pass them and I see air-conditioned bubbles with neatly dressed foreigners, and I don't like them. It isn't out of envy so much as they seem like voyeurs, even to me. Yet here I hypocritically sit, squashed and cramped in the hot, crushing taxi, while being loudly ignored by the fat woman sat next to me. I am also a foreign devil, a white invader in their midst.

Throughout the journey, the driver has subjected us to a loud radio that squeals and whistles as it picks up local mosque prayers broadcast through distorted loudspeakers via cheap microphones. There is an intense cultural immersion happening in my chosen mode of transport, and I am engaging in it rather than just observing it from a distance. Though I'm sure the fat lady would have preferred it if I hadn't come. I don't much like the overbearing and insulting manner that is typical of being a tourist, and even though I am guilty of being one myself, I dislike the role. We rarely try to fit into a place, we just drive on through other people's backyards, staring at them blankly from within our rented, bubble-vehicles. Ogling at their freakishness compared to the way of life that we know. We remain aloof, demanding, entitled, and invariably get stroppy when we don't get what we want. We will spend vast amounts of money just so we can be full of expectations and take every minor error out on waiters, waitresses, and menial hotel staff. All the while acting as if we own the entire world, although in fairness, some of us probably do. I don't blame her for hating us.

On the second leg of the plane journey out, it had come as a surprise to see that a lot of the passengers had been middle-aged white women travelling alone. Almost all of them had something of an superior air about themselves, and no one seemed to want to engage me in conversation. I found it odd that they seemed to prefer to ignore me. I wondered if it was because they knew I was judging them, or because I was a white male and they were out there on the hunt for some Nubian youth, so I didn't measure up. Why else did they come out here? I didn't ask, but I think I guessed it correctly after seeing some young local boys here running around with older white ladies, eagerly attending to their needs. And now here I am, just another one of the rank-and-file backpackers, another two-bit European low-life doing it on the cheap. Dead-set on invading Morocco how I want, and not necessarily how they prefer I might. I guess I am in no position to judge anyone.

I tire of the long car journey and soon nod off to sleep. The car hits a bump and I bounce awake, disturbed to discover where I am. I'm trying not to fall asleep on the fat lady's shoulder, as I think she might stab me if I do. After what feels like an eternity, we arrive in Zagora just as my watch hits midday. I alight from the taxi to stretch and then go to find somewhere to eat and relieve myself.

It's getting hot. My super-fly, high-tech, funky watch shows thirty-one degrees on the temperature gauge. Then I hit a few buttons, and it tells me I am at 624 meters above sea level.

I decide to chill out for a bit and recover from the Grand Taxi experience, which I have to admit was an ordeal. Finding coffee and toilets in a café opposite the taxi station, I order up two *café noir* and hoof the first one down.

An old man accosts me soon after I sit down and have taken out my notebook with a plan to write. I had not noticed the flies until now, but they are out in full force in Zagora and pester me, too. The old fella is sweet, a little scrawny, but he produces two ornate and lovely looking daggers that he wants to sell me. When I say no, he asks for money for food instead, motioning towards his mouth. I know not to give it. The guide books have been specific about that:

"Do not encourage the ways of begging, it is not a good means of survival for either party in the long run."

The wording I find curious as it implies I might die if I give money to beggars, which seems serious, so I take heed. The old guy has me tempted, but I resist. Before he can work to charm me further, the waiter sees him off, thus solving the problem. But the flies remain, and they come at me mercilessly.

The sun moves a shadow across my table as I scratch pen to paper and write. Soon breaking my shade, the giant yellow orb then turns to burn down right on me. I like the feel of it at first, but I need to be careful. I'm still lily white from a long English winter. Moving out from under its radiating glare, I decide it is time for me to eat, then take another leak, and then put on some sun-tan lotion. After that, I need to find a taxi to take me the rest of the way to M'Hamid, or get a room for the night somewhere here in Zagora.

Just Keep Calm And Carry On

In Zagora, I get my first Moroccan meal at a place I see the locals are eating. It's nice grub, a beef Tagine, and it costs me thirty-one dirham. After eating, I go to get a taxi. I am eager to get to M'Hamid and find a way out to the desert from there. I go first to get a bottle of water, having struggled during the morning taxi ride without one, but events take a detour after entering the shop.

The guy who serves me is wearing white camel-hair slippers, and they look ridiculous. The white tufts of fur are curling chaotically over the top of his dark brown toes and from a distance they stand out, making it appear as if he has huge furry feet. He is immensely proud of these things, but I can't stop laughing at them. Pleased with their effect on me, he then switches from being a humble Moroccan, struggling to understand my requests, to speaking perfectly good English. I stand with my jaw hanging down at this sudden switch, trying to figure him out. The gall of the man to be wearing such outrageous footwear is one thing, but his sudden and unexpected change in behaviour is a whole other peculiarity. This leaves me curious to know more, and I think he knows the effect works on tourists to disarm them. His next question now has me engaged, and it is to ask me why I am visiting Morocco. After I tell him, he is eager to take me to visit his brother, whom he says can offer me cheap camel rides into the Sahara desert where I can stay with the Tuareg desert people who live out there. Initially, I am happy to dismiss him as a rogue and stick to my plan, but something about his incongruously gaudy footwear and his obvious intelligence keeps my interest. I want to know what else I might find if I let him lead the way.

A short time after, and we are walking the back alleys of Zagora, which also looks like a middle-eastern city after a bombing raid. I have a sudden attack of irrational fear, *what if hairy camel-toe is leading me into a trap*? I work hard at suppressing the paranoia that is growing stronger the deeper into the back alleys we go, but before long we cut back out onto the main road, and from there we enter Camel Tour shop. Inside I meet his "brother", though they don't look related. They summon tea and we sit down around the brew on comfortable cushions as my first Moroccan sales ceremony gets underway.

First, the brother shows me a book of not very inspiring photos, and then a guest-book full of past testimony as to his illustrious worth. I'd been sold on the idea already, but I play along to familiarise myself with the Moroccan way of things. Friends who had experienced them before had warned me about these tea ceremonies. Those same friends also had a bet on that I would inevitably buy a carpet, but I felt confident my money was safe.

I was never very good at haggling, and I blame my private education and middle-class British upbringing for that failure. It taught me to be polite to everyone at all times, to agree with everything even when we didn't, and to do this for the sake of good public relations and the ongoing maintenance of stoic appearances. Today we mock this behaviour with the familiar adage *Keep calm and carry on,* but it has its roots in some very real and culturally ingrained behaviour. Despite years of rehabilitation on the streets of London, I never could shake it when I needed to the most. Moroccans, I am rapidly discovering, are the Scousers (Liverpudlians) of Africa and I don't mean that in a derogatory sense, only that they seem overly eager to help me part with cash for things that I don't need.

I am offered the bargain deal of five hundred and fifty dirham for one night's stay in the desert with food, tent, and the camel ride included. This prompts me to check my travel bible - *The Lonely Planet Guide Book* - which says upwards of three hundred is standard. I consider trying to haggle it down but I can't be bothered, I'm convinced these guys are genuine. Assuming that my money will go to the locals rather than to some European business set up, I'm happy to go with their set price. I agree to pay the five-hundred and fifty, since it's only about forty quid. They look disappointed with the ease of their sales success, and I soon discover why I should have haggled.

A pause ensues during which they pass odd looks to one another and then say some words I don't understand, before teaming up to insist that I go with them to another shop. I'm unable to make them understand the word "no". I'm soon being led out of the shop and down the road. Moments later we're in another boutique where I am met by yet more Moroccans, and we get down to drinking more sugary tea and another sales pitch begins. This time they show me jewellery and carpets while telling me all about the Tuareg history and the traditions associated with each item. I don't recall asking for any of this, but the tea sure tastes good and everything feels delightfully foreign. I'm happy because the one thing I wanted to achieve - a night in the Sahara desert - I've found and booked with hardly any effort at all.

I nod politely at the array of wares brought out for me to look at. I remain firmly dismissive, but it doesn't stop them as they hit me with deal after deal, item after item. They pause only briefly to top-up my sugary tea before returning to the onslaught. It's a whirl of retail dervishes, their banter drifting away from pidgin English and further into Moroccan. My eyes are glazing over and my mind is swirling, as yet another carpet appears and dances around in front of me. I notice a sinking feeling. I'm getting tired and feeling ever more badgered and flustered by their histrionics. There is an overwhelm occurring, and through the noise and the chaos, my mind throws up a red flag. I'm being lured into something here and no amount of disinterest on my part is working to stop it. The more disinterest I show, the more effort they put into trying to sell me something, anything, possibly *everything* in the shop. I'm desperately looking around for ways to escape, or for something to distract me from the endless bombardment. I spy a necklace with the Tuareg alphabet inscribed on it, which reminds me of Mayan symbols that I've seen before. But showing interest in anything is a fatal mistake. Deals are now afoot to sell me three bargain items, along with the necklace. The sugar rush is peaking and I have a sense they know how my mind works better than I do. It's just a matter of time before something else grabs my attention, and they are looking out for it. The dog is on the rabbit, and the rabbit is getting tired. The pace of the sales pitch ramps up a notch, though I didn't think it was possible, they achieve it. It's a method designed to abuse my senses until I can take no more, and it's working.

I'm getting close. There is a relentless savagery happening here, as a variety of new items are being thrust at me, on me, over me. The tension is increasing to boiling point. Their babble pierces the air in a crescendo and cacophony of chaos. It's deliberate. It's a barrage. It's shock-and-awe. A consistent attrition and targeting of my senses until I break.

Just then, a glimmer of clarity appears to me through the haze of the sugar high and above the indecipherable babble of their loud and foreign voices, and I grab at it. What the fuck do I need with a Tuareg trinket, a mid-sized carpet, an Arabian outfit, a life-sized stuffed camel, and a brass tea set with matching cups? How was I even getting drawn into this nonsense? I see sense, finally, and I put my foot down.

"NO MORE!" I shout, "Please, gentlemen, just stop!"

And it's just in time. I was about to part with seven hundred and fifty dirham, plus shipping, for a bunch of crap just to get them to shut up. Instead, I settle for a small headcloth to make a turban out of, since I haven't brought a sunhat and will need something for my trip into the desert. When I try it on later, I discover they have sold me half a turban and wrapped it up to disguise the fact. I guess they felt miffed. They so nearly had me for much more.

They can tell that it's over, and they've failed to cajole me into larger purchases during the window of opportunity. In a synchronised motion, all the men sit down, lean back, and then speak conspiratorially to one another. Some of them do so without exchanging looks. If someone asked me to guess what they said, it was derogatory, racist, and a lot less friendly than one might have hoped for. I realised they had known exactly how long the sugar rush would last for, and just what kind of window they had to batter me - an unwitting, fresh-off-the-boat tourist - into submission. It had nearly worked, but there was no way I needed or wanted any of that stuff. I was travelling too light to carry anything, anyway. The Moroccan support team then disappeared, and that left me with the original two; hairy camel-toe and his alleged brother. They both then take to clicking their tongues in light disgust at my refusal to spend more money and ignore me while discussing ways to improve on their methods in the future.

Good old British guilt pangs hit me, but a wave of anger follows, at the insolence of strangers treating me like an ATM. A sense of indignation rises in my throat, and I have the urge to unleash a tirade of abuse against my hosts. How very dare they treat a British subject in this way! But then I consider whose fault that is. I'm just another tourist on the conveyor belt to Morocco. It also dawns on me that without other tourists around I could be out of my depth to pick a fight in their shop. I decide it best to just keep calm and carry on, so I sit there smouldering, while I slither down the anxiety side of a sugar crash.

We stay in the shop for a while longer and they continue to talk to each other in Moroccan, and then hairy camel-toe and I head back to the tour shop, and from there he takes me on a moped ride to the taxi rank. Once there, he hands me a slip of paper with some Arabic writing scrawled on it, along with the verbal promise that a man will meet me at the other end. I wait in the heat and the dust until my next Grand Taxi fills and is ready to go.

We leave Zagora at 3 pm. I am concerned that I might not make it in time, and further anxiety arises at the thought that I might have just been duped. I try to ignore the feeling. Duped or not, it has been a hell of an experience, and in its own way, it was quite fun. It only cost me a small amount of money, and I am now headed towards where I want to be. If I have any problems, I know where to find his shop again. So, I allay the fears and focus on surviving the Grand Taxi ride, which is jam-packed and as crazy as usual.

An hour and a half later, I arrive at a similarly named Camel Tour shop just before M'Hamid. I am met there at the side of the road by a desert guide with a dry and pock-marked face, dressed in a stunning turquoise cloak. With hardly a word said, I am helped out of the taxi, hoisted up onto the back of a camel, and we are off into the desert towards some dunes.

Camels are far more comfortable than I had imagined them to be, and it's an hypnotically peaceful journey as we set off into the golden desert and the graduating late afternoon light. We talk little with the language barrier between us, but a brief and amusing episode ensues when I ask him what animals live out there in the desert. Since he can't explain them in any language I can understand, we communicate using animal noises instead. We gesture to each other using the movements they make and with shadows on the ground, which adds a curious dimension to our game. A Salvador Daliesque scene is created in the landscape as the low angle of the sun hits the long legs of the camels and throws distinctive long shapes onto the sand canvas while the creatures lollop along in slow motion. It's as mesmerising and fun as it is communicative and engaging, and it's a great way to bridge the tension created by our inability to speak the same language. When it turns out that there aren't many animals in the desert to mimic, we move onto whatever animal we can think of and imitate it for the other to guess at. I like my guide. He's fun and has a cool and low-key manner, though I imagine him to be a man who prefers the silence and quiet solitude of the desert, and I can relate to that.

Another hour further on, as the sun sets over the dunes of the Sahara, we arrive at three tents and I'm helped to dismount. We stand looking at one another, neither of us able to say anything and making stupid noises no longer seeming appropriate. He doesn't have any desire to advise me on what to do next and just stares at me. No one else is around that I can see, and after some awkward loitering, I make motions to suggest that I wish to have a look about. He affirms that it's fine to do so with a wave of his hand, and so I head out towards a nearby dune the height of a house, for solitude and a view of the setting sun.

I can't quite shake the tension that's gnawing away at me, there is the added fear of now having to socialise with someone I can't speak a word with. I'm tired from the long day, but alert from all the excitement. It's only been twenty-four hours since I arrived in Morocco, and yet I've already made the journey I thought would take me three days. I am deep in the Sahara desert. Miles out amongst the dunes, and a million miles away from the modern world I'm so boringly familiar with and desperate to escape. Everything here is a scene straight out of *Lawrence of Arabia*. Time has stopped, reversed even. The Bedouin tents, the Tuareg dress, the camels, and these perfect golden dunes going off in every direction to the horizon. It's an old-world lost in time, and yet I have found it within a day or two of departing my office desk in London. It doesn't seem real, and I can hardly take it all in.

Tuareg

It's easy to get disorientated out amongst the dunes and as soon as I step over the brow of one, every direction looks the same. I check my watch and compass, wondering how easy it would be to find my way back to the tents if I wandered off and became lost, and conclude it would be hopeless. It's a joy to be alone in the desert, but I'm uncomfortable with the prospect of the night ahead, which will no doubt involve a lot of communication difficulties and awkward silences. I'm the only tourist staying out there and from what I can tell, there are only two men at the camp. The tents look lived in, and I wonder if it's a permanent camp or a mobile one. I stay on the dunes for a while longer, keeping the tents in sight, but before darkness falls, I head back. The men are in the smaller of the three tents and I brace myself for a confusing experience.

I stay up with my hosts until after 9 pm. We eat and drink and I meet other suitably dressed Tuareg desert men who drift in at various times. I'm now convinced this isn't just a setup for the tourists, but is how they live. We spend the time struggling to understand one another and I feel a culture-shock in being there amongst them. My animal impressionist guide hardly speaks, and I think we would've been happy making animal noises for the night, or just sitting in silence and not trying to make any sense at all. A later arrival is a young man, maybe in his twenties, and he speaks the best English of all of them. The older men are mostly quiet, while the younger men are given to brash outbursts and laughter. I don't feel a sense of disdain coming from any of them, not in the way I experienced it from the "sales team" in Zagora. I feel respected and welcomed here, and they're not interested in getting me to part with money. Rather, they seem fascinated by me, and their eyes glow and glisten in the candlelight as they watch me intently. The new arrival is especially interested to hear about my life and asks me many questions. We take turns asking about one another's world, and he translates my replies to the others. They all live such a different way of life that I find it difficult to find a common ground between us - nothing I can speak about at length - and so the conversation stutters on subjects that have no meaning to them. They don't do any of the same things that I do, and our worlds are so very different that inevitably the subject soon turns to the one thing we are all curious about - women.

They tell me that in Morocco you shouldn't speak to a woman unless it's your wife. To get a wife requires money, or for you to have a perceived value of some sort. I take from this conversation that Moroccan women exist to be bartered and are prized like horses. I'm then told that none of the men in that tent will ever have wives, and that thought takes me aback. What a strange life it would be without women. I try to imagine it and conclude that these guys don't have a hope in hell. I can't fathom such an existence. This also explains why western women are the holy grail to them, and I soon discover that they have idealised them in all the wrong ways. Once they realise that I'm open to the conversation, all they want to talk about is western women. I try to steer the conversation away from it because it's painfully awkward, given how they seem to think. To some of their enquiries, I don't know how best to respond. They're like children asking questions about the complexities of Quantum algebra, and they laugh at the most immature aspects. I realise that it's taken me years of exposure to the mad creatures to have even a basic understanding of them. Where do I begin? I feel the discussion is beyond me, and I'm uncertain of the effect my more obtuse comments might have. So, I attempt to bring it all back around to discussing Moroccan culture instead. I want to learn more about what I'm experiencing out there, but I've unleashed Pandora's box, and whether I like it or not, I've just become the chief representative for western women amongst a small gathering of Tuareg men. I fear this won't go well for either party.

The differences between their way of life and mine have me humbled. I was not expecting it to be such an old world or quite so impoverished and archaic. This way of life should be a thing of the past, at least for the young men, but this seems to be their lot. For men to have no access to women seems bizarre to me too. Whenever I stop sharing information, the younger men talk amongst themselves. I get the impression they are assessing all I have told them and weighing it up against their existing group assumptions. I also surmise that they rarely get the chance to talk openly about women with western men, maybe because many men come out here with their partners, or women are present on most tour trips.

The young men chain-smoke cigarettes and continue to joke loudly, but I am soon getting tired. I don't want to seem rude, but I want to enjoy some solitary time before bed. The desert has been calling me to soak up the experience, and I wish to do that alone. I try to find a polite moment to exit, but the conversation comes back to women again, so I give it one more round.

They are unaware of the trappings of the west, and don't understand the world that I live in, or rather, they believe in a peculiar version of it. I can understand why they think how they do, and also why they are inquisitive to know more, especially about the workings of the female of the species. What man doesn't wonder about that mystery? But from what I can gather, they have painted my world into an odd mix that lands somewhere between a Utopian dream and a joke. I'm not sure they have a very high regard for us, either, nor for women in general, but I put that down to a lack of any proper exposure to either. They are not rude, just blissfully unaware of the facts as I know them. I get the impression they believe we lounge beside swimming pools all day, have lots of cash and servants, and get sexually serviced by western women that have an insatiable appetite for sex, never need consent, and are all stunningly beautiful and large chested. All I have to do is to grab one and she will be willing. My new Moroccan friends want to hear all about *that* version of my world. They no longer want to talk about desert life and make that clear. I guess I can't blame them for that. I wonder if seeing MTV videos in town bars has reinforced these ideas, because it all sounds a lot like a scene from a trashy R&B music video to me.

At first, I am not sure if I should ruin their delusion. If I were to tell them the truth, would they have believed me, anyway? Given how I feel about *their* lifestyle, it seems insulting to tell them I am miserable in mine. How will it sound if I say that my life sucks, that I feel like a slave to the economic machinery of the west, or that western women are... um... complicated? How can I tell them the very reason I am out there is to ask them about the romanticised lifestyle I have imagined they live in the desert? I can't bring myself to ruin their dream. The one thing they all seem to enjoy the most is the idea of the existence of insatiable western women. What if that is the thing that keeps them going through those lonely, male-only, desert nights? Who am I to tamper with that kind of hope? So, I give them the stories they want to hear. Some are true, and some are slightly exaggerated, but one thing is certain - the wilder they are, the more they love them. I'm like a goddamn hero by the time I leave for bed. And having done my part to set male-female relations back a few hundred years, and feeling certain that I have now stayed up long enough to be polite, I find a gap between the questions and bid them all good night.

When I get to my tent, I prepare my sleeping bag on the soft rug that's on the sand there. I am in the centre of an area big enough to hold thirty people and could still leave room for dancers and a bar. Dancers and harems. Just two of the many things that I had imagined existed out there, but it turns out they don't. There are no women here. I, too, have received an education this night.

With the tent to myself, I lie down and stare up into the soft canvas roof for a while. I am not ready to sleep just yet, and after letting myself relax and unwind from an animated evening spent with the lads, I throw caution to the wind, get up, and walk out into the desert night air. Being careful to put markers in the sand so I can retrace my steps.

A bright moon and a billion stars light the night up. It's

odd how electric light makes the night sky seem darker, but once you escape the cities and towns, it's light enough to see, once your eyes adjust. I walk until I can escape the noise still coming from the tent of my hosts, and that takes exactly one dune. When I walk over the brow, all noise disappears. The sand is a superb sound-proofing material. In an instant, I am a million miles from anywhere and on another planet. Mars, maybe. I sit myself down on the silver-blue carpet in a dip between dunes and wonder about things. I look up at the bright twinkling stars on what is a beautifully clear night. It is a fantastic feeling to be immersed alone in that world and is worth every bit of sweat it has taken me to get there. I lie back on the sand and consider the day's events.

It saddened me to hear of the disappearing Tuareg ways. Not only is it being challenged from the outside, just as all indigenous people seem to be, but they long for something they believe exists somewhere else. They think they want my world, or their version of it. I had hoped to find an ancient culture that had no interest in western ways. Instead, I find them idealising it, almost as much as they mock it. I want indigenous people to be immune to us, but they are not. I also learnt - from our brief sashay into politics - that the disputed Algerian border now blocks their livelihoods. They can no longer trade how they once did, and it leaves only tourism for them to make a legal living from. I got the impression that my Tuareg hosts would see little of the money paid to Hairy camel-toe and his alleged brother. The young men smoke a lot of cigarettes while the older ones don't, and the young men talk of women, drink, contraband, and business ideas. Though it is more bragging than a workable reality from what I could tell. They have little idea they are losing a tradition by desiring to escape it, and they seem to have little concern for the gradual loss that is occurring to their way of life. Young, trapped, and bored; they want out. The young men want the world they think I come from, the one in the stories I embellished for them. They want sexy, wild, lascivious women from R&B music videos. They want the success and riches they imagine exist in England. As if it is all just low-hanging fruit that we pluck from the western tree of plenty. They want a delusional dream. They want the very thing that I have just run away from. Our worlds are so far apart that it leaves me confused. Their longing actually mirrors mine.

When I left their tent to head to bed, they all followed me out. I then asked about the stars and navigation, but it was clear they knew little of it other than to give a tourist the impression that they were wise in traditional astronomy. I asked which way was north, thinking they might have some canny method for devising it, but they didn't know. So I pointed it out to them. How come I knew more than they did about the constellations? It was odd, since they lived under them. So I pointed out Orion next. I was interested to hear their thoughts on it. They knew that one, and I was told how they called it The Man, and to his right was The Dog which sits between The Man and The Woman, who was a little further to the right. They said that The Man was forever chasing The Woman across the sky, which seemed like a fitting place to leave it, given the dominant theme of the night.

Something was slipping away from all of us. It wasn't just out of our reach, but seemed to be disappearing from the world as time passed. As I stood there in the desert night with the last of the Saharan Tuareg, or maybe they were just shopkeepers doing a good impression of it, either way, I knew we were all doomed. And I'm not alone in this sentiment. There are many men in the west, just like myself, born with a feeling that something is missing from our worlds, our cultures, and our souls. We all feel a lack of purpose and a loss of meaning because of it. Some of us go searching for answers, and we come to these places hoping to find them. But when we get here, we only ever find other men, other worlds, different in so many fascinating ways, but underneath it all, we are all caught in the same dynamic - we are chase that elusive feminine energy across the skies, in whatever form she might manifest for us. We are chasing rainbows. We have a longing, an emptiness that needs to be fulfilled. In the absence of any kind of solution, that emptiness gets filled by dreams and ideologies, ambitions, or beliefs. Failing those things filling the hole, then we seek drink, drugs, or even religion. None are more than a blanket of delusion that hides an insatiable and vacuous hunger that can never be satisfied. We may stick labels on presumed solutions to our longings - *women, jobs, cash, ambition, political ideals,* or *Utopian dreams*. Whatever we think will give us the answer, we then go looking for. Driven by a desire to solve something that we can't even properly define. It was in that moment, stood outside the tent with the Tuareg people and looking up at the stars, that I realized that the indigenous world didn't have the answers I needed either.

The fact that ye olde desert men didn't know which way North was, had thrown me. I wondered if they were genuine, or had simply been sent to provide authenticity to my trip. All around the world, our indigenous knowledge and heritage is vanishing. Our connection to the natural world is like a light that has been dwindling and will eventually go out. We are becoming ever more disconnected from nature and separated from the earth beneath our feet. The earth being the source of place we spring from. Now, we have become used to living in bubbles, separated from the realness of a direct existence. This has created a longing within us. Implacable and indescribable, but powerful and impacting none-the-less. The absence of proper connection has created an insatiable hunger within. Culturally, we are becoming more isolated, yet we are doing this together. We are driving it there. To most of us that might seem meaningless to dwell on, hippy drivel of the highest order. But maybe it's necessary to look at it, in the same way an illness requires finding a matching medicine to heal. What medicine could satisfy the hunger in our souls? What is it we are missing, really?

Consumerism has filled the hole where religion might have worked in days of yore. Before that, indigenous ways would have met it, by honouring life in daily rituals. Our accumulating sense of grief, was dealt with rituals to our ancestors, and ceremonial gifts made to the "gods" of our environments. Ritual in the community is how we would have connected to the world we mutually exist in, as well as to each other. Indigenous cultures talk to the land together; to the animals, to the gods, and to the spirits. They also talk to their ancestors, and they create a personal bond to a place, and to each other, by doing so. That act then becomes sacred, as it fills the day and adds a sense of reverence to our acts. And that sense of the sacred is what has become lost to the west. Nothing is sacred to us any more. We have become insatiable consumers instead. We have become isolated. We live in our bubbles of disbelief. Maybe remembering those ways again will be what reconnects us, not just to the world outside of us, but to each other, and ultimately, to ourselves. That kind of sacred communion found in ritual can feed our hearts with a love and a warmth that we are currently lacking. We become fed by engaging in connection to whatever we perceive the creative forces to be - Science, God,

Allah, Spirit, our ancestors, or even the Void. These are all just words to describe aspects of the cosmos that surrounds us. But they remain indefinable, eternal, and infinite. The descriptive words of ancient indigenous people, their spirits and their gods, are no different to modern-day concepts described by Quantum Theories, or in Science. The only difference being that our ancestors talked to those forces and treated them as living entities, and in doing so, they created a connection to them, directly and emotionally. They personalised them. And by doing so, they filled the gap we now feel is a void, a longing, and a vacuous hunger. This is why modern man feels disconnected; he no longer talks to the world about him as if it were sentient.

In modernity, we have learnt to drug our pain into oblivion and we prefer to become numb to avoid experiencing any grief. Living in cities and towns, we become cut off from the connection to the earth and to nature. Slowly, inexorably, we enter the machinery of modernity and are digested by it, then evolve along with it. This legacy is noisy, and powerfully distracting to our senses. Modernity is a machine that numbs our pain, demands our attention, and before we are fully formed as autonomous thinking beings, we have become unwitting slaves to it, led there by our guardians. Before long, we can't exist without the soporific numbing effect that the machine has upon us. Plugged in, it feeds us and sustains us, but only if we work *for* it. To live outside the machine is now impossible, but it's the very reason I sought the solitude of the desert.

I have run to the furthest point to get away from the belly of the machine, to run away from everything in my world that serves to distract me. I came out here for just a moment to catch my breath and escape it. All this, just to find a place to slow down long enough to feel a sense of stillness. To recall it, and to engage it. That is why we come to these places - we are seeking stillness. But it's not that easy to cure the problem, because we can't grasp it once we find it. We cannot connect to the stillness we seek. Where we require it to exist, is inside of us. We have forgotten how to become still. Not moving, not thinking, and existing without any internal distraction. The machine has our complete allegiance, we carry it with us, and it lives on inside us. To make matters more difficult, the moment that we do start to become still, then fear and anxiety arise to make us move again.

I'd hoped to find an answer to my questions here in the indigenous world of Africa. I'd hoped it would be here waiting for me somewhere at the edge of this continent. That I would discover it, and in doing so, I might find purpose again. I wanted to find an explanation for what I was missing and maybe an answer for *why* it was missing. I had secretly thought it would be easy. That it must still be alive and thriving in the heart of the Sahara and its people. Surely the desert would remain untouched by the machine of modernity. And that the further south I went into Africa, the wilder it would become, and so the greater chance of discovering some magical solution waiting for me here. I don't think I am the first explorer to make this mistake.

Instead, I'm left with the painful awareness that it's faded from these places too, assuming it ever existed. I don't need to continue on deeper into Africa to know this. Our direct connection to the spirit is broken. Everywhere on earth it has happened or is happening. The world of nature, the place where the spirit belongs, is being overrun by concrete jungles, luxury flats, and bubbles of existence that encourage a television-fed, machine-dependant, drug-induced existence. The more dissonant we become, the more separated we become, and the more empty and hungry we become. We have all become disconnected. We're already blind to the true cause of our longings. The modern solution is *consumerism,* but the more we consume, the more we hunger. I wanted to find the joy of stillness and solitude out here in the desert, but I found the Tuareg and their longing for the false-lights of the world of modernity that I had just briefly escaped. This tells me something. And I discover that I'm at the face of the mirror.

I remain out alone in the desert night for a long time. Feeling tense and uptight after the rigours of the day. I find the stillness I was looking for, but from it, a miserable feeling arises and envelops me. I think about my life, and how well things have gone for me, at least on the surface. When I compare my life to that of my hosts, I don't feel I have the right to be miserable, and yet that is exactly how I feel. I am diabolically, shamefully, woefully miserable. Then it shifts and morphs and gives way to a feeling of being utterly alone, not just in the desert, nor in my life back home, but by the very nature of my existence. It makes me feel tiny and inconsequential to be feeling it in the desert night. The immensity of where I am, and the awareness that in any direction it just goes on forever, leaves me perplexed by my feelings. Why haven't I noticed how big it is before? But what hurts the most, if I am honest, is that I have no one to share the moment with.

Being out here gives me perspective, and I consider how I have deliberately become numb in my life and am no longer awake to my situation. I've spent the last couple of years disconnecting from everyone and everything. Like a functioning zombie. I am present, yet not present at all. I've been lying to myself about this for a long time. Telling myself that I will change one day when I figure it out. I have been kidding myself that my life has meaning. My friends, people around me, the things that I concern myself with each day, none of it has any value to me. I am not interested in any of it. Everything that I do is empty and driven by a need to avoid admitting to that fact. I'm busy doing nothing. And just so long as I don't have to face the vacuousness of my existence, I can pretend I don't care. I am not happy with my life, but I don't know what else to do, so I fake it.

I feel even more lost in the desert than I did back home. It is like being lost in space. I feel pitiful for being able to conjure no other feeling than a self-centred misery in such a beautiful location. But it is also useful. From so far away, lost deep in the dunes and looking down at my life, I can see myself for the fraud that I am. What am I doing with my time on earth? And how much longer am I going to give myself to work it all out? I wonder when I first started lying to myself, and I suspect that I have always been doing it.

A desire to travel came late in life for me, but it has now come. I am not happy with life in London any longer, where once I was content just to flow. Travel seems to wake me up enough to see that, and so it is a start, a beginning to my re-awakening. Travelling feels better than staying still, and that means travel holds a hope for me. A hope that I might somehow figure it all out, if I can just keep on moving. I've been drifting through life for several years, but my inertia has now trapped me in one place, unaware, until recently, that stagnation was occurring because of it. I've been vaguely aware of it happening, but I numb it with drink and drugs. This method is no longer working for me, and it's why I hit the wall. It's the first time that I don't know what to do to change a situation, and that's why I looked to travel for a cure. Whatever I tried, failed to resolve it, but travel has brought me opportunity and excitement, which is something. And that is why I am now out here in the desert. I am looking for an answer to my emptiness, and a direction to head in next.

I yawn and realise that I am at last tired. I am getting no further with my reverie. So, I take out the same small bundle of items that I brought with me, the same ones I used on the first night to make my prayers and thoughts to the ancestors, and I lay them out on the blue moonlit sand. I speak my thanks and give gratitude to the powers that have helped me to make the journey to be there, and to whatever made me plod my way out into the desert that night. It would've been just as easy to go to sleep instead. And I feel like it is a good thing that I am aware of my struggle, even if I don't know how to resolve it yet. I'm grateful, and I want to be grateful, and that's something that makes me feel good. The misery dispels as I talk and offer my thanks. There will always be opportunities coming towards me, even if I can't see them yet. They must be there, and "the gods" and my ancestors will lead me to them, or vice versa. I'm following something spiritual by making this journey. Reconnecting to it from within by making this libation. It's a start. I'm attempting to punch through the headwinds that were set against me. It is a pilgrimage I am on once again. This time it was to the Sahara desert. This trip has been an opportunity that I dreamed into being, then dared to make happen. It feels important to know that I have called it to happen. To risk everything to come out here, to be here now, and to call to the unknown from this remote and solitary corner of nowhere and nothingness, just a place of sand and silence. I know now, for the first time since I had the idea, that I've done the right thing in coming.

I sought out the most far-flung and distant point that I could reach in the time that I had available. To then signal my intentions to stop feeling sorry for myself and move forward with my life. I need to prove myself, maybe just to myself. I've made it to the solitude of the Sahara desert in North Africa. It is a good place to be, and to make this kind of wish. I am at the outer edges of my existence, somewhere unreal, unfamiliar, and unknown to me. It has shaken my being loose. Now I conjure a thought, an intention, or whatever one might call it - a prayer, maybe. And I hold it up to the powers-that-be as a small sacrifice and gesture to show my willingness.

Though I haven't found what I had hoped to find here, at least not amongst the people that inhabit the Sahara, it still felt right to come. Maybe it has some relevance of its own that I don't need to fathom. And maybe I don't need to have a reason for being here, either. I made a mistake in judgement, sure, but I also learned something from that. Mistakes are educational. I followed my intuition, assuming at the end of it there would be an answer, some sort of convenient reward like an easy pot of gold. What I found were other men reflecting on the same longing that I have, only theirs is mirrored. It turns out, that at the edge of the world there is a reflective surface.

I am just another man on a journey through life headed towards the inevitable, and just like everyone that goes before me I am wondering what it all means. We all struggle with our anxiety, our emotions, and a sense of meaninglessness. We all spring from a mysterious source that no one understands, and we are all headed towards a beyond that we understand even less. All I can do is give gratitude for the opportunity to be here asking questions. And what else is there but the journey? To reach out towards something that I can't see or sense with any certainty, and to ask for help on it. There may be nothing out there. My prayers just a gesture made towards emptiness, for all I know. Whatever has been going on with my life of late, it required that I head to the most extreme point of my journey, and to the very edge of my universe to reach out for answers from there. Because if the thing I need is going to be anywhere, then it is bound to be just beyond the farthest point of my reach.

Kasbah

I sleep well, though I wake feeling cold. The dawn light shines through the holes in the cloth tent above me and I lie there for a while enjoying the fact I'm in the Sahara desert. Getting up at 8:30 feeling invigorated and refreshed, we eat breakfast in the same tent that we'd talked in the night before, and I spend it with a friendly cat sat on my lap. The sadness of the night has lifted, and I feel more amiable and chatty. Mornings are always a positive time for me; the day ahead fresh, untouched, and somehow hopeful. Someone comes in, and I'm told to finish breakfast quickly because a sand storm is on its way. There's a sense of urgency to get going before it arrives. Everything happens at a quick pace, and before I have time to think about it, I'm being hoisted back up onto my camel and off we go.

We conduct the return journey in a pleasant silence. It doesn't feel rushed, which I'm glad about. I had visions of galloping on a camel in a race against time, but it was an easy stroll, though faster than it had been on the journey out. After an hour or so, we arrive back at the edge of the small town of M'Hamid and the spot that I'd started out from. As I dismount, I can see the sand obscuring the skies some distance behind us. The turquoise-clothed Tuareg, my friendly desert guide and award-winning animal impressionist, nods at me and then hovers close for a moment. I'm adjusting to being back on solid land, stretching, and thinking about the coming sand storm, wondering if I need to be concerned. Another guide is there waiting who speaks very good English, and he tells me he can take me around a local town if I wish. I thank my turquoise Tuareg desert friend with a handshake and he then leaves. Soon after, I realize he was hovering in the hope of a tip. I feel terrible for not thinking about it before, but it's too late now. It would be pointless paying it to my new guide in the hope he would see any of it. It's an unforgivable mistake on my part and I'm annoyed at myself for making it. The very people who deserve the most often end up getting the least.

I am shown around a Kasbah at a place called Oued Draas, which is in the next town on the road back towards Zagora and far enough away that we miss the sand storm [Though I cannot find Oued Draas or anything like it on a map later, it was only a short drive from my camel pickup point in M'Hamid]. My new guide is a well-dressed Moroccan who has the look and way of an educated man. He is friendly, young, and his English is good. The Kasbah is amazing. It has a homely feel with its earthen style architecture and close-in, high walls. I wish I had a camera with me when I spy a woman and donkey walking up one of its enclave tunnels silhouetted in the light at the far end. It would have made a picture-perfect postcard. My guide tells me how they made the Kasbah, its layout and the reasons behind the design of each room, but that's as far as my interest goes, and my attention span too. I'm a terrible tourist, preferring to find my own way through places, but I'm polite and grateful for his guidance. The tour ends at a shop where the usual sales shenanigans begin. Here we go with the sugary tea, again. This time, they dress me in various Tuareg outfits. The intention is to make me feel I should buy one just for wearing it. I'm polite and go along with the enforced charade, but disrobe at the end of each attempt and stand waiting for it all to be over, and for them to realise it's not going as planned.

I'm the only European in town again, and I've seen only Moroccans since I left Ouarzazate. This makes me feel my being here is invasive, and it feels wrong to be donning their cultural dress. I'm being made to feel uncomfortable. It's as if I am supposed to part with money to feel better about it all. I want to object because this is making me feel like a clown, but I bite my tongue and smile through the experience. There is a temptation to tell them that some people just aren't into buying this crap, but they need the money and this is all they know, and I'm sure it works well with most tourists. I remind myself that we have created this problem, so we now have to live with it. We are the greedy, consumptive, trophy buyers. My detached disinterest confuses the shop-keepers, but I don't expect them to treat me any other way than this. Eventually they give up making me try on outfits, and then they move onto carpets and jewellery. Of course they do. But I'm getting wiser to this process now. Unsurprisingly, I see the same stuff I saw in the other shops in Zagora. The same "authentic" products being wheeled out and held up for me to admire. I remain disinterested and after this round they give up a little quicker. I finally get to leave without having purchased a thing.

With the shopping finale now done, I'm taken by my guide to wait in the town square for a lift onward, but my next taxi only goes as far as Tagounite. There I find another taxi, but have to wait for it to fill. While I wait, I am accosted by Omar, who is the spitting image of Antonio Banderas, though poorer, more desperate, and possibly mental. Then a young lad joins him called Mohammid, and he's trying to become my new best friend, too. Neither leaves me in peace, even when I take out my pen and notepad and sit down on the kerb to write. They continue to find things to distract me with, and at their insistence I make a promise to include them in what I write and we confirm together that I've spelt their names correctly. I get enough of what I need written down and then give up thinking they'll leave me alone. I announce that I wish to buy them both tea as a reward for their determined persistence. The wrong thing to do, maybe, but one can only take so much.

We sit in a nearby café to drink and they want to know how to get educated in England. I tell them England holds nothing they imagine it to, but they don't believe me at all. I don't know which of us is correct, but they seem happy to spend the time telling me how England *really* is. Eventually, I am rescued by my taxi leaving.

It's the little things you miss recording down as you tear across Morocco on a mad adventure. Small but intense incidents happen so quickly and so often that you can easily forget them as they pass you by. Then, before you know it, the next one is upon you and requires all of your attention. Grabbing the rare and brief moments I'm left alone long enough to write, I try to recall them and put them to paper before they are lost forever. Here are some more:

Last night in the desert, I was trying to capture the mood as the silence descended on the tent during a brief pause in our chatter. I had a moment to look around me, take in just where I was amongst the desert people of the ancient Tuareg camp. I felt trapped in some kind of impervious bubble that just wouldn't seem to pop. So I shut my eyes, and the Tuareg talked amongst themselves. I felt into the place, sunk my attention into the earth below me and tried to get a handle on the unique wonder of the moment that I found myself in. I wanted to know it intimately, trying to tap into the reality of where I was. Out there in the Sahara desert, in an ancient world and way of life. Could it get any more real than that? I opened my eyes and looked around me at the bedouin tent, these strange foreign men, and the desert home that was so alien to my way of living. It nearly sank in at that moment. I could almost grasp it. I'd escaped the machine, escaped my cultural normality and travelled back in time. My bubble was wobbling and shimmering. It was about to pop. Then the sound of *The Dukes of Hazard* theme tune blasted through the tent and all the men pulled out their mobile phones to see whose it was.

Grand Taxis are an experience not to be missed, and I recommend braving one should the opportunity arise. Passing convoys of comfortably air-conditioned RVs while you sit squished, butt-aching, in amongst at least six sweaty bodies has its own unique kind of enchantment. It was unexpected to find a curious enjoyment in that experience. I suppose it came from the knowledge that I'd be leaving within the week and would be back to relative luxury soon after. Maybe that's what made it an endearing and worthwhile experience to have. But the journey back from Tagounite to Zagora took it to new levels I wouldn't have thought possible if I hadn't experienced it first-hand. We arrived with not six, but eleven people crammed into our car. It was ridiculous. Even some of the local passengers thought so, too. I could not see a window, nor move a limb, for the last twenty kilometres of the journey.

There are police checkpoints at random spots along the road that all the taxis have to slow down for, but they are often just waved on when they do. A defined military presence makes itself felt in Morocco. I am uncertain why they pull taxis over when they do, but as we reached Zagora, a lone military man stood by the side of the road flagged us down. He had chiselled features and a stern expression, and I assumed the driver was about to receive a fine for overfilling his car, but no, he just ejected one man from the front-seat scrum and then got in to ride the rest of the way to Zagora. Unsurprisingly, he didn't have to pay. I suspect from their manner that beneath the pristine military exterior there lurks the heart of a nasty bastard. And I won't be testing this theory if I can help it.

Having touched down briefly in the dunes of the Sahara and after spending a good amount of time body-to-body with the natives of Morocco, I eventually find myself sat back at the cafe in Zagora. This time it is with a sense that I am now getting to know the heart of the place and to acclimatise to it. It has been a shock, and a fast, heady lesson in the workings and the ways of an alien culture. Alien to me, at least. What I liked the most about the desert people was their mild manner, their calmness, and their open and obvious kindness. There was no hint of suspicion or distrust there. This makes me aware that I feel a certain distrust of most people, not only in Morocco, but in humanity.

People in the towns here cling onto you, they attach themselves. Which is overwhelming for a Brit used to keeping himself at a decent social distance. I've had to learn how to be stern while remaining polite, but they won't leave you alone if they sense an opportunity. They look for an angle, a way in, as much out of interest to know you, but always, ultimately, it's aimed at getting you to part with cash too.

I try not to fall for the begging ploy in any country, and I consider each time that I refuse to be a good thing. The guide books are very clear on this, especially regarding Africa. The beggars, and shopkeepers, will hit you with every kind of trick to keep your attention, and they know what they are doing. In Morocco, it begins with getting you to enter a conversation, which may be followed by the generous offer of tea to help keep you there. After that, you're hit with a deluge of endless sales spiel. It's attrition. It can get annoying, because no sooner do you escape one than another accosts you. Ignorance doesn't work either, and nor does outright off-handedness. I've also tried playing dumb but to no effect, and getting angry would be a foolish mistake. Something *must* work, but other than developing leprosy, I'm not sure what would shake them off. Tourism creates the problem, and in fairness, they are not unfriendly, they just don't give up easily. The more I engage with them, the more I find most of them to be charming. In conclusion, once I relaxed a bit and let down my English defensiveness, I soon discovered that Moroccans were well worth the time and effort to get to know.

Animus Est Solvo

It's 3:20 pm on Monday. I'm still in a café in Zagora and considering wild-camping and whether it will be workable out here. Outside of the town there are only bare rocky outcrops, and everywhere else - like the walled fields around Zagora - there are people wandering around and they seem to spend a large part of the day there.

I am considering all the risks of trekking out into the rocky desert beyond the town, all the things that could go wrong and how to deal with them. As I'm thinking through the possibilities, I allow some kids to grab the remnants of my food from my dinner plate. They get some and scarper off before the waiter can spot the crime. I'd seen them creeping up, knew what they were up to, and turned away just long enough for them to take their chance. Subtly pushing the plate in their direction to let them know I'd finished. It's becoming increasingly difficult to follow the rule of not giving to the beggars. Asking for money is one thing, but kids being hungry is another.

After a little more consideration of the wild-camping risks,

I decide to save my energy, and rather than head out there tonight, I'll go tomorrow night instead. This means, that for the rest of today and tonight I can relax a bit. The pace has been pretty dazzling so far. I recall more events and jot them down in my notes.

The taxi journey on the way to M'Hamid was spent listening to the radio blaring out with what sounded like a Hitler speech. It was Germanic, intense, and aggressive. This wasn't the usual mosque "sing-along", but an angry rant. It persisted for the entire journey and made for a bizarre soundtrack. With me being the only foreigner in the car, I wondered if I should be concerned. I couldn't make out a word of what the voice was trumpeting, but after an hour, it became like a river of curiously eloquent beauty to me. Despite the anger, the architecture of the words, the voice, and the way it expressed emotion became fascinating. The sound was punching my ear in the way only Germanic staccato can. It was loud, abrupt, sharp, and guttural in its delivery. With a lack of comprehension, it instead caught me in its auditory flow and I became immersed in it, hypnotised almost. The nuance of the emotion it carried, held me entranced. The expression of it was everything. There was such an intensity driving it, and he was clearly feeling very passionate about something. I felt I was being mesmerised, and I wondered if that was what made an orator excel in the art to do that. It was like a torrent of violent water hitting my senses. The fast flow of a gushing river. I had a feeling that my people might well be the subject, which added a curious uncertainty to the experience for me. Was everyone in the taxi being schooled in the evils of western culture? It was bizarre to be amid that experience while being unaware of what exactly was being said. I checked for potential assassins at one point, but no one seemed roused to war as far as I could tell. It was just another ride in a Moroccan Grand Taxi where everyone looked bored and kept themselves to themselves, despite being packed in so intimately.

On most taxi trips, we experienced the tinny car radio blaring Moroccan or Arabic music. Sometimes there were African songs with voices singing over twangy electric guitar solos that crudely followed the melody. Most of these had the vocals painfully over-produced, at least to my ears, with the voice stamped on heavily by an auto-tune effect that made it sound ridiculously false. I don't recall hearing any western songs on these trips, and I liked that. It was a new cultural experience that I was getting.

I've detected an element of political and racial tension in the towns and sometimes notice an offishness from individuals in the cramped taxis. Like with the woman who didn't want to sit next to me and made a point of letting everyone know about it. Current affairs, ancient cultural and religious differences, and our basic ignorance of one another's ways have all had an influence on this sense of division existing between us, not to mention the language barrier. It's sometimes overt, as they have no reason or need to hide it here. I guess it comes as a surprise to discover other countries can be racist too.

Earlier, I was making my way up the main road in Zagora and some teenage kids were passing on the other side. I thought nothing of it until one of them pulled his hand across his throat while staring at me, and it was not subtle. I suspect he did it to impress his friends more than to threaten me directly, but it was clear what it implied. There's no mistaking a gesture like that. So, I stopped walking and held his look. The ignorance of it irked me, and I saw no excuse for doing it. I also felt I had a responsibility not to ignore it. Threats of that nature made when travelling alone in a strange land have to be taken seriously.

I said nothing and made no retaliatory gesture in return, choosing instead simply to observe him from a place of stillness. I maintained a neutral position, but was preparing for whatever engagement might come next. It would do no good to get annoyed, but neither was it wise to turn away from a situation out of fear. Better to face into it calmly, I felt, but also to plan a response and method of escape should it escalate. I felt certain that it was just teenage bravado, but I needed to be sure. And by presenting a willingness to go the distance if required, he might reconsider doing such a stupid thing the next time he met a tourist. I waited in a relaxed pose and held him in a soft gaze from across the street, but he knew what was implied by it. I was giving him the opportunity to engage me. His demeanour changed then. I don't think he had expected to be confronted, and he looked away nervously. Other than a cursory look shortly afterwards to confirm that I was still standing there watching him, he didn't turn to look at me again. I decided from this response that he wasn't a threat, but who could say for certain? Someone had just implied my throat should be slit.

It left me a little upset, and I wondered what would help to build a bridge over the chasm that exists between cultures. I blame the media and our politics. But teenagers, I long ago discovered, are ass-holes in any country, and are always best avoided. A bit like venomous snakes; where the young are the most dangerous because they haven't yet learnt a reason *not* to bite. Maybe it was nothing to be bothered about, but it could easily have been. And though I have experienced far worse on the streets of England, my fear and uncertainty are more sensitive and alert for trouble out here. Anywhere we go in the world, there will be someone who doesn't like us, even if it is for no reason other than just *because*. Most of the time it's not personal, they just don't know who, or what, we are about. Their experience comes from a narrative that they have taken on without thinking, just the same as we have of them. I'm as ignorant of Moroccans as they are of me. But as a solo traveller, I have to figure out how to deal with abuse or threat when I come across it, and I need to do so without inviting further trouble. I know from experience this isn't something I'm good at. I'm not the diplomatic type and will often stand my ground belligerently, but that can lead to confrontation. But to run away or show fear is to invite an attack, especially from young men. I risked shaming that boy's sense of pride by standing there and facing him, and that might then have forced him to prove himself.

Somewhere between responding directly, versus ignoring people, lies the solution. I dislike ignoring it because it feels like I am being given an opportunity, and to some extent, a responsibility to address it. I believe we should face into it, not avoid it, but with a certain amount of common sense and discretion attached. De-escalation is difficult, and remaining neutral or calm in a situation is difficult. I am better at causing fights. Staring at him, observing him as I did so, I stood my ground, but all the while thought about how I would manage a confrontation if it came to it. It didn't come, but I think it left him considering the same thing, which hopefully will give him pause before doing it again. And in that, it left me feeling confident that the biggest fear for a Moroccan teenager would have been threatening to tell his mum about his behaviour.

I leave the café and continue on up Avenue Hussein II, avoiding the camel shop but looking for a campsite that I've been told also has a swimming pool. I eventually find the campsite *Sinidbad*, but it's small, and the pool is empty of water.

"Too early in the season," I'm told by the owner.

So far, this is the only disadvantage I've found in visiting Morocco before the summer months. The weather is more than perfect. My watch read thirty-five degrees in the desert as the sunset yesterday evening.

I head next to campsite *Les Jardins De Zagora*. When I get there, the boy at reception tells me they have no campsite. In my late afternoon daze, I feel tired and can't be bothered to pick up my rucksack and move on again just yet, so I stand there taking the scenery in for a while and my mind goes into neutral, locking on a daydream.

I'm staring at the large rocky mountain back-drop behind Zagora. *Jbel Zagora*, I believe. It's away to the east, and it draws my tired attention as I wonder whether to give up with the official campsites and just wander out that way until it gets dark. I stand there for a while longer, pretty much dumb to the outside world and dribbling a bit. An adult comes out of an office and asks how I am doing. It turns out they do have tent areas after all, and I am taken to see them.

They are small, square, four-walled affairs in a row of five, all made from concrete blocks with hessian canvas thrown over the top to act as a roof. Scaffold poles hold the canvas up in the middle of each section, and the floor is of a levelled concrete. It's not a camping area as I am used to seeing them, and looks more like a place where bins might be kept, but it will do for tonight, and it's clean. It's still too hot to relax in the concrete shed even with the hessian roofing, so I leave my stuff at one, and then go for what I realise is a desperately overdue ablution. I have swallowed a lot of sand during my time in the desert, and though the baby-wipes I've brought are a blessing, it's a sand-paper experience that I could have lived without.

Les actual *Jardins* are opposite my tent but they all look dead, and beyond them is the open-air restaurant where I now relax to write. The boy who was at reception is here now too, and no longer on duty. He skins up a reefer, lights it, and then offers me some, but as always, I politely decline. I undo my boots and give my feet some air. It's nice to be out of them. There is a circular fire-pit in the middle of the garden and I stare at it. Once again sending me off into a daydream. The discolouration on its walls appeals to me. I'm seeing faces and shapes in the pebbles that jut out from the exterior. I recall how I saw faces in the desert as we crossed it on the camels. It was hypnotic being out there, and it had a strange effect on the mind. After a while, I began seeing spirits presenting themselves from the desolate terrain as we rode through it. And more than that, it felt like the spirits of the desert were coming out to have a look at *me*. Even the shadows seemed more alive out there. Such distinct and sharp edges made them jump out of the uniform golden sand. It was mesmerising to watch my guide making animal shapes with his shadows. Desert puppetry. Alive, and in motion. The shapes had distinct defined edges, and from the height of the camels they became giants on the sand. I was watching dream-like images come to life against a golden canvas in a setting that was already odd to be in. It hadn't struck me until now just how weird that entire trip had been. The shadows opening up a secret world that they then drew me into. It felt to me as if they emitted information from their blackness, made more intense by the bright light of the desert under that sun. It presented a void that one could dive into, and the mind somersaulted on into another dimension. Shadows holding information we are usually too busy to notice. It held a language of its own. Whatever information was in them seemed to be in a state of flux, emerging from the landscape engaging bubbles of emotion that I could then observe in myself. It was like being left speechless by fine art, but it felt more alive and connecting, because the shadows moved and had a flow. I couldn't tell you what kind of language it was, maybe the language of the desert. It felt like a communication that I was once familiar with, but had forgotten. In the desert, there is nothing to do but hallucinate and to dream while wide awake. I sank into that aspect comfortably and naturally, maybe in part because I was so tired and mind-blown already, but I became captivated by it, and soon was waving a gentle salutation to whatever spirits appeared and caught my eye. Beings, creatures, whatever they were, out there *where the wild things are*. I let the dream-state take me over, and it happened with no resistance from my mind. It was a relief to fall into it, and it felt so natural that my mind hadn't questioned it until now. There seemed to be no pressure out there, no reason *not* to let go. There was no learning required, nor initiation of any sort to achieve that coveted state. It had occurred all by itself.

I play my tongue around in my mouth and I realize that one thing I am missing from my kit is a toothpick. I risk getting ill from poking my pen tip into my mouth in my attempts to dislodge the meat strings that are stuck there after the recent tagine. This prompts me to list some items that I should get for future trips. Soft toilet paper for blowing dust and mucus out of the nose. Though it's not essential, there is never any paper in the toilets here. The toilets are porcelain holes in the ground with what looks like the base of moon-boots moulded into the concrete for one to stand upon and squat. To the western mind, such positioning feels uncivilised, but I have read that the design of the human body is such that it makes it the superior position to perform the essential movement from. Maybe *we* are the heathens.

The wind sprang up suddenly on the return journey from the desert camp, though the expected sandstorm did not arrive. And though it wasn't uncomfortable with my wrap-around shades on, the sand dried itself onto my face, leaving my lips cracked and the skin on my face feeling raw, which it still does. I noticed how aged and craggy the faces of my Tuareg hosts were. I can confirm that daily bathing in sand, sun, and wind does the body no favours.

Now that I'm relaxing, I'm again made aware of how a nagging discomfort exists within me. It has been especially intense since I arrived. Though it hums away in me most of the time, it grew stronger in the days before I left to come out here. It's an ache, a tension, and I can't exactly explain the source. I had thought it was because of my years of drug abuse, but it amplifies in situations such as these, which makes me wonder about it now. Straightforward anxiety, I guess. Though it's more the sense of being *in* my body that aches, rather than my body itself. It's an odd feeling when it becomes intense. I don't think it's always been this way, but is certainly something I have to live with now.

Last night in the desert, when sadness and misery seemed about to scupper me, I recalled the necklace that I carry as an identity tag when I go on my solo adventures into the wilds. I only wear it on my travels to places where, if the worst should happen and they might not find my body for a long time, then identifying my remains would be easy. It's not out of morbidity, just a sensible precaution. On one side of it, I have my UK National Security number etched into the metal, and on the other I have the words, *"Animus est Solvo"*. It was supposed to translate as *"the soul is free"*, but I admit not checking it properly before getting it done at a cobblers in Harrow one rushed lunchtime. When I eventually got a Latin expert to confirm it, he translated it to more properly mean *"the mind is loose"*.

But the recollection of that discovery freed me last night from the desperate loneliness that I experienced out there. I felt so lost and alone in the vastness that it really wouldn't make much sense to explain it more than I already have. Thousands of miles from home, bodily, mentally, and historically, it had a big impact on me. And it was the simplicity of that necklace - something of no real monetary worth, just a flat piece of tin on a cheap metal bath-chain with some words etched into it - that brought me a sense of comfort and solace. Something so simple, and yet can be powerful enough to shift our mood. It warmed my heart to recall those words, and the silly sentiment I had so humourously failed to capture, it made it almost medicinal.

I'm pretty sure one could go mad left alone in the desert for too long. It almost seems made for it. I imagine the same thing must happen to astronauts when they look back at the earth from space. In that moment, one would realise just how easy it is to become detached from humanity, when turning around points you at the ultimate loneliness of the Infinite. *The soul is free*. I played the meaning of it around in my mind. Home, is really just a feeling that we carry inside ourselves wherever we travel.

I'll be giving my military-grade hammock its first test-run tonight inside of my hessian-covered concrete campsite. The scaffold poles holding up the tent roof seem secure enough to take the weight, and it affords me the chance to get a feel for it before heading out tomorrow to the desert to put it up between palm trees, assuming I can find some.

I head back to the camp area and set about the task, and within thirty minutes, it's up. It seems bizarre to be doing it inside of a walled area, but the hessian cover holds no real protection from a sudden rainstorm, so there is some sense in using it. Now I can sleep easy, safe from bugs and rain should either come in the night. I'm not sure of my plans tomorrow, but in the restaurant I scoped the mountains with my monocular and saw palm trees up there.

After satisfying myself that tonight's setup is good to go, I head back to the restaurant. It's still empty. Alpha Blondy plays on the best stereo in Morocco with a heart-warming bit of bass, finally, and not the tinny whine of cheap car radios. There's not much to do tonight, nothing much to see, and it's too quiet to expect the garden fire-pit to be lit. I sit around in the restaurant for a while as the sun sets. My watch tells me it is twenty-six degrees. There's no sign of a tan on my skin, and it's feeling dry, which makes me think I should have brought fish oil tablets out with me, and I add them to my list for next time. But that damn annoying ache is still in me.

A mosque hails somewhere distant. Its tannoy starting up and the familiar voice of the disciple calling a monotheistic and young religion to prayer (young compared to animist beliefs). God, Allah, what are they about? I have had little time to seek out my own gods since being here, other than briefly last night in the desert and the night when I first arrived. I don't go in for the monotheistic faiths any more, and they make no sense to me at all. Animist beliefs make more sense, along with Science, of course. Animist belief resonates because it embraces the original, spiritual attention given by a man to the natural world that surrounds him. We have likely practiced it for hundreds of thousands of years, if not millions. And during that time, it never needed to change much. It's always offered a simple way for man to communicate and connect directly to the spirit of the world that he finds himself in. It's a way to engage the personality within all things. A way to connect to the essence of anything. And it's straightforward. It's the same in the tribes of Africa, as in the tribes of South America, or in Asia, or in the Himalayas. Anywhere the indigenous still survive, you can find the essence of it. It needs no middle-man begging for our prescriptive allegiance to a one-god system, nor our money. We can find a personality in anything, and in doing so, it permits us to engage with it. A human, an animal, a tree, or even a rock. Giving them personification gives us a way to connect with them at some level. The rituals of animism give us a way to connect to the cosmos, with our feelings and with our grief, and that seems important, since it is all we really have. And since I don't believe in spirits or gods, scientifically speaking one might instead refer to such things as *energy, force, mass, dark matter, the cosmos*, or whatever. It's just different definitions for the same things that animist belief systems labelled in their own way, specific to the time. It feels more honest and direct for me to engage in the universe directly, and I can do it at a personal level with animist beliefs. For me, it works.

While monotheistic organised religions - all of which are only a few thousand years old at best - were designed for controlling the masses. They seem to have been built with that intention, and cater to the needs of the few in their quest for power. Creating a middle-man who then sits between the disciple and his, or her, god, is a convenient way to control people. When humanity left the small tribal groups that would have indulged in a more animist connection to nature, the powers-that-be had to maintain control of those larger groups. What better way than with a set of "commandments" applied using stories that created fear, shame, or guilt, so that people then policed themselves and each other. Organised religions became power structures that benefited only certain people while controlling the rest. None of them seem all that genuine, and all of them demand an illogical, unquestioning faith. Once it became about *one-god*, then the choice became to accept it, or being killed. Organised religions run a neutered, falsified, deliberately warped and violently imposed narrative, and I have no more faith in their literature than I put in a Harry Potter book. They are a similar fiction, and none stand up to logical questioning. When people go misty eyed over claims of their god as the *only* one, I know them to be lunatics. Religion reflects what is wrong with the world today. It's a mania. But I guess people need something to believe in, and we all have a right to choose for ourselves what we think that might be. I choose animist beliefs and science, because together they make sense of the universe for me and with those two tools, I can connect to it better and find my place in it.

The Stars That Guide Us

[I wrote the first six lines of the song "Ride Across the River" by Dire Straits here, but I can't share them because of copyright, so you'll just have to imagine.]

It's Tuesday morning on the 7th March. Singing as I break camp is one of the best feelings. The night was an interesting experience and one that proved to me it's a good idea to test a set-up before throwing myself at the mercy of the elements. I got into the hammock at about 9 pm. I was dressed in a thermal jumper and boxer shorts, and I tucked myself into the sleeping bag to find warmth. The wind had whipped up as soon as the sun went down, but I felt snug, and the hammock was great, even becoming too hot at one point. My mind meandered over my trip and a warm glow of happiness washed over me. I was doing it. I was travelling solo and into the wild. Adventuring again. Pushing my boundaries, escaping the rat-race, and getting abroad for the first time in over two years. At that moment, I couldn't have been happier.

Not long after coming back from the trip to Spain - that I wrote about in *"The Road To El Palmar"* - I left my partner of seven years and sold most of my possessions. It took a while to get used to being single again. It also left me floundering in a city and a lifestyle that I no longer seemed to enjoy and in which I now feel trapped. Despite being more than happy in London for nearly twenty years, the love affair has waned. I can feel the hard concrete beneath my feet with each step I take, and a lack of direction seems to consume me with an ever-increasing sense of self-doubt. Working through the days, I booze and drug myself through the nights to compensate for loss of direction. I'm looking for relief, but that behaviour is not helping me to find it. My life feels like it's on an endless washing-machine cycle. I'm going round and round, always exhibiting the same symptoms, while remaining devoid of any real purpose other than to get high. It's a spin cycle on repeat. At the weekends I seek bland, sexual dalliances and drugs. I want nothing serious to weigh on me and drag me back into the world of relationships. I am still caught in the whirl of mind-numbing endless partying. It was what I loved about London when I first arrived there from Oxford in the late eighties; London was a twenty-four-seven party town that supplied me with everything I could ever want or need, but I was a young man back then. And though it's nice that all of that is available to me still, it's been wearing me down these last few years. I'm not only unsatisfied with the lifestyle, but I have a feeling it is now killing me. I keep thinking I should love it, but I don't enjoy it as much as I thought, not really. I have become a fraud and a caricature of my former self. Each weekend is leaving me in a deeper mess that I find harder to recover from. And for the last few years I have been doing stupid things when high that I'm not proud of and find hard to explain when straight, even to myself.

So, a vacuum has been growing in my soul for some time. My nature-loving spirit has not been getting fed, my skin is sore from psoriasis, and my forty-year-old body has started to creak and complain in ways that I never thought would happen to me. So, I'm showing signs of getting old, and I'm not dealing with it at all well. I thought I was Peter Pan. It hurts to discover that I'm not. The youthful glisten in my eye has dulled. The reason for my continued existence is, at best, confused. I'm lost in space. The plot has escaped me. Charm replaced by simmering anger that has become a subtle, growing resentment at my lot, and my failure to change course has disarmed me further. I'm annoyed at myself for ending up like this. I had assumed that I would have much more going for me by now. I thought getting older would be easier than it is proving to be. It's a tale of self-pity, I know, but it's true. And that's why I came out here. I want to break the neck of this thing, and to re-invigorate some part of myself, or maybe just find the strength to accept that I have lost the game.

Last night as I lay in the hammock, cosy, tired and mulling over the last few days, I considered all that I've achieved so far on this trip. Daring to take a leap of faith into my fears, I left England and headed out into the unknown alone, and went further than I am used to doing solo. I am still alive, so far, and though it has taken a long time to stop feeling terrified, there is also a platform of calm assertiveness that I've found to stand upon, and I feel great about that. I've done something. I've taken an enormous risk, and it has worked out well. I *am* having a good time out here. It means a lot to have got that right, and I'm regaining some of my lost confidence by acknowledging it.

As my hammock swung gently from side to side, the night-time wind occasionally whipped up the hessian canvas above me. The movement created interesting shapes with the crescent moon that seemed to dance there, its light making shards with the bright white beams that shone through the holes in the material. Then I glimpsed the two stars that I had seen from the plane, the ones that had looked to me like the eyes of a snake-god.

I'd become obsessed with snakes as a kid, and I felt an affinity towards them long after the first time I encountered them in Africa. Later, when we moved to Portland in Oregon, I would go hunting them in the fields around where we lived. I was only ten or eleven, and was determined to catch a rattlesnake. I had an intuitive knowing for snakes back then, a fearless awareness of them and a fascination, a certainty that I understood them. It was something indicative of a deeper echo in my spirit that drew me to seek them out. Where had that natural affinity come from? Today, I don't know, and I no longer feel it the same as I did back then. It had terrified my parents to discover I was hunting rattlers, and my dad had to give me a serious talk about the dangers. I knew the risks, but I remained unafraid. Sharks and spiders terrified me, but snakes were just something I seemed to feel familiar and at peace with. As much as my dad was happy to see me engrossed in something that interested me, it concerned him I was hunting for the aggressive and deadly version. He tried to encourage me to focus on garter snakes and other harmless breeds, but every time we got out of the car on a road trip, I would be off to the nearest rocks or gully to look for rattlers. I caught many snakes in my time, but the rattlers evaded me, and everyone was glad of it but me. When I reached my teenage years, girls soon distracted my attention and within a few months of losing my virginity, I forgot all about snakes. I don't think I have considered them again until this moment.

As I lay under the watch of those two stars, I wondered - was it a memory that I'd carried into this world that had drawn me to hunt snakes, or had I been a snake in a past life, or maybe I was going to be a snake in a future one? Did it all mean something, or did it all mean nothing at all? Looking through the roof material as I swung there, and seeing those distant eyes watching me, I was remembering the bond I had with them. Through the veil of the world, it now watched me from the other side. Our connection forgotten, but not lost. It was calling me to seek it again, but in a deeper way this time. The spirit existing in worlds beyond this one, outside of our universe and beyond physical form. The rattlesnake, a protector, a truth teller, a witness to the journey, waiting out there as part of a bigger picture, beyond time, and in a place that has no beginning in birth nor ending in death, and a place where fear no longer has meaning, a place beyond *Time*.

I fell asleep at some point and then woke to hear what sounded like dozens of desert dogs barking, and I lay listening to their call. They were howling out to one another, like a night-time telegraph system speaking in the tongue of the wild.

Whenever I become immersed in nature, what comes with it is a sense of being alive in the moment and allowing myself to enjoy it rather than be annoyed by it. It happened on the last trip and it was happening again now. It's nourishing to have that awareness, but it is not always a comfortable experience. Often it has a catch, and a bite that jars us out of our amnesic state for a price that is often pain. I've been so long in the city that I've forgotten how good it feels to be out in the wild and a little more exposed to the elements. The daily grind in routine rubs away our connection to nature. A different kind of survival is required for us to live in the harsh but clinical and sanitized world of modernity. It's a world of concrete, with statically charged air caused by the exhaust from electrical devices. Endless sounds from machines that click and hum around us all day and all night, helping to keep the hermetically sealed environment in exactly the right conditions for comfort. The grinding of cogs in the wheel, as it turns and develops into ever more powerful machinery meant to serve us, but also domesticate us. The hammering of building developments amidst the raging scream of hot fossil fuelled engines that drive our world to function. Those are the sounds that rule the machine-dominated cities of our era, and they repel nature.

By tapping back into the world of nature, I am tapping back into an ancient spiritual well of life. Coming out here, it connects me back to it again, and it didn't take long this time. There is always a risk we face in doing it, and maybe it's supposed to be that way. We should feel a bite of pain when plugging back in. Nature can just as easily devour us, even kill us, if she chooses to. She is mother to us, but she is also a cold and ruthless hunter, and she *will* feed on us if we give her the opportunity. She is both loving mother and savage killer rolled into one. There are no rules of engagement she has to obey, and her beauty and mystery lie in accepting that paradox. I wonder about the quality of what feeds me at this moment, and why it is missing from our cities, why we fear it after we spend a long time away from nature. It comes back to us when we become exposed to the night, or to the desert, or to the wilds. When we reconnect with nature, she nips at us and it takes a few bites to wake us up. She is dangerous, and yet that quality brings us back to life. I am now in a country that hums with her heartbeat. I could feel it in the desert and I can feel it here in the Zagoran night. The emptiness of the Sahara is nothing like the emptiness found in a first-world city. The desert is more alive.

Part of what reawakens that awareness is by becoming free for a while, by avoiding living according to a schedule. Then we can follow her call. She was calling to me through the howl of those dogs, and it gave me a strange sense of knowing something as I listened to them. They had regained their awareness of being part wolf, and I could hear it in the sound and the feeling it carried. Their howling was a call to the wild. Through it the wild came to meet *them* and in that moment they escaped their domesticated prison, and in listening to it, I did too. I fell into the dream. My meandering thoughts that flowed and felt wholesome to dwell on were available to me again. No one to laugh at me, or question my thinking, or to shame me and call me a fool. When I let go, I could sense something else present within everything, and it is *that* which feeds the wild in us and we reconnect through it. The filter of the rational mind falls away, and we feel comfortable to let that happen. I didn't shut the connection down like I normally would. I remained still, did nothing, and allowed myself to be enveloped by it, and so it carried me away along with it.

I thought again about the rattlesnake spirit. I was seeing through the eyes of the stars and they shone into my imagination. They became *my* eyes, and with them I was observing myself. Watching the story of my life unfolding here on earth. Why was this connection impossible in the city? Why was it absent from the world that I came from? Why did I fear it and feel shame for feeling it? And why was it so easy to find it out there in the desert? Was it Africa, or Morocco, or the desert, or the land the brought it back to me now? Or was it the people that somehow kept it alive by not concreting over it and modernizing everything? Maybe it was just the time in my life that I had come to. It made me feel that something was missing and that I needed to reconnect. I was at a crossroads again, that much was certain, because I could feel it right there.

I could have stayed awake all night conjuring odd thoughts and listening to the wild barking dogs, but I also knew it would be better to do so the next night, once I was in the desert outside Zagora. I had known all along that I needed to escape into the wilds, to escape the familiar surrounds I had grown accustomed to living in. It felt like I was waking up again after sleepwalking for the last two years. I'd heard the first heard echoes of it on that trip to Spain, and there was an inevitability to it back then too. It had awoken an urge in me that would no longer rest. And now I was heading out into yet wilder places to seek that awakening again.

But there is another side to this story that I can't deny - As much as I am trying to find something, I am running away from something, too. Running from the trappings of my rational mind and the world I know, I am trying to get away from myself, and that may be a fool's errand. Maybe going alone into the wilds of the desert is not the best way to achieve what I am trying to achieve, but what choice do I have? And it seems to be working.

The Persistent Breeze

After the barking dogs, I fell asleep again, and awoke at 2 am shivering with cold. A soft but persistent breeze had entered the sheltered area, and with my back against the thin material of the underside of the hammock, it was robbing my body of warmth. I couldn't grasp what was happening at first. I was so chilled that my mind was foggy, but I knew I had to move despite the inconvenience, and I didn't feel so great. It was hard work persuading my mind to get my body to function, but eventually I roused myself to action, and once I was out of the hammock I felt warmer. The movement brought me around, and I slapped my body trying to conjure a more functioning wakefulness. It made no sense why it had become so cold in the hammock, as it felt warm enough when I was outside of it.

After a while trying to warm my core up, I got back in and wrapped everything around me again. Only moments after settling back in and becoming still, it happened again. I felt the barely perceptible breeze biting into my back and draining me of warmth. I got back out of the hammock. What the hell was going on? It wasn't all that cold, and yet the persistent breeze could not be ignored. Barely noticeable, it was like a subtle lick of breath, and yet it cut the heat right out of my body in a short space of time. It felt deliberate, malevolent.

I stood in the concrete enclosure for a while, thinking about how best to address the problem. I was still shivering, despite not feeling all that cold outside the hammock, it had got through to my bones. Everything around me was pitch-black apart from the stars that still peeped through the holes in the sackcloth above my head. My mind wasn't working very well, and at some point I realised I was mumbling incoherently.

"It's a survival situation, it's a survival situation."

I noticed the words rolling out of my mouth. I guess I was trying to remind myself that I needed to do something. The surprise at discovering that I was talking gave me a jolt. I wondered if I was losing the plot. Though it made little sense that it could happen at a camp site in the middle of town, it was happening. I gave myself two hard slaps across the face, and the pain did the trick. I was immediately awake and thinking more clearly. That brief episode had been strange. The chill had been numbing me out. It was a reminder of the true nature of things, and of how a perfectly safe situation could turn harmful if left unchecked. So what to do?

Well, first I needed to figure out what was giving me a problem, but I already knew what it was - that peculiar malevolent breeze. I also knew the solution. *Insulation* was the key thing missing from my setup. I could have wrapped up in a hundred blankets and that persistent breeze would still cut through and suck the heat from my bones. Lying on the bare ground would have had the same effect, sucking the heat right out of the body, and I knew this. What I didn't know was that the breeze could have the same effect when in a hammock. This was new information for me. I grabbed my torch and as soon as I turned it on, the bulb blew. Yet more drama.

I was glad it happened though, and I was glad of my decision not to venture out on that first night. I'd just had a wonderful lesson in preparation, and it happened while in a relatively safe environment to experience it from. Had it happened out in the desert's wild night, it would have compounded my problems dramatically. Luckily, in this case, the shelter had a light, and so I fumbled around until I found the switch and turned it on.

The solution to both my problems presented itself in the form of my rucksack. Within it was my back-up torch, which immediately went higher on my inventory of things to have handy before nightfall. I already knew the rule of survival was to have two of everything, and now I had an additional rule: *to make sure I knew where they were before darkness*. And the solution to my second problem - that of the cold eating into my bones - was my rucksack itself. It had an insulation layer of foam padding where it sat against my back.

Later on during the journey home, when I was staring mindlessly at the information monitor on the aeroplane, I noticed that the temperature outside at 37,000 feet was at minus 74 degrees. It made me wonder how we stayed warm on a plane. Minus 74 was pretty damn cold, and yet I could see that the window protecting us from that low temperature outside seemed to be very thin. That intrigued me. So I made a closer examination and saw there were three layers of thin plastic between us and the outside. An air-gap separated each one. It was the doubled-up air-gap which provided the insulation from the cold outside. The cold would draw the heat away from what was inside, but the air-gap provided a layer of insulation, and two air-gaps made it work much better to defend against the temperature discrepancy between outside and in. I also noticed that the middle piece of plastic had a small hole drilled through it at the bottom, and I realised it must be there to enable the pressure to balance out between the two zones. It was a simple design, yet beautifully efficient. I took a note to consider it later. Warmth, but insulation specifically, could be the difference between life and death in the wilds on a chilly night.

The simplicity of those windows in a plane of such complexity struck me as being almost a magical thing. Someone had invented it, and I wondered whom? And how had it come about? It made me consider the many achievements of humanity. How much we have discovered, learnt, and passed on to the next generation who then improve upon those designs. All of it comes from a desire to create a better world for the rest of us, and to make a more comfortable experience for those that come after. We accumulate this legacy like a shared diary, and we write this story into all our technological inventions. Some of them are so simple and efficient we barely notice them, and yet the job they do is often life-saving.

It meant a great deal for me to realise that. I had often stared out of plane windows and had never considered them before. And it is in these small, yet barely noticeable inventions, that the entire journal of humanity is to be found. More than that, I felt certain it was a sign of the essential goodness of human nature in our innate desire to help one another. Despite our well known homicidal tendencies, deep down we care to improve our lot, not just for ourselves, but for others, and in doing so we seek to make headway in that endeavour. We have a desire to leave a legacy of lasting value. Yet each new generation takes it all for granted. We can't help it, because are unaware of how much has been done for us. We never try to imagine how much harder life would be without each item we make use of. It's only in moments like these that they come to light.

And just as with those air-gapped windows, any part of the plane I was in - as it whisked us across entire continents in relative comfort and safety - was a miracle that we took for granted. As much as it was fantastic for us to enjoy these inventions because they made our lives easier, it also made us ignorant of what went into them. Such convenience of living makes us numb, and as a result we become given to higher expectations. Our chances of survival have improved, as have our levels of comfort, and yet in correlation to that, so has our ignorance and disinterest.

I had never considered it before, and I had never thought to be grateful for it, either. I decided, on the spot, that I needed to change that and become more appreciate of the small inventions that I had never paid any attention to. And if I had not written it down here, I would never have remembered that grand gesture.

So, with my rucksack laid out in the hammock to protect my back with a layer of insulation, it did indeed save the situation. The breeze still woke me, but it now licked around the sides of my hammock and reached over the rest of my body instead. It was still drawing the heat away from the top of my sleeping bag, but with my back insulated, I was warm enough to get back to sleep and stay there. After that, I fell into a set of unexpectedly debauched dreams, and I awoke at 8 am to feel the life-giving warmth of the morning light breaking through. As the light grew stronger, so the wilfulness of the cruel breeze seemed to recede in correlation to it. I felt it had been seeking me out all night, but with the daylight, it had been banished.

Having survived the night and now knowing what to expect, I felt ready to head out into the wilds outside Zagora for a proper test of my will, skill, knowledge, and ability to survive, even if only for one night. The test-run was complete. Tonight would be the real deal.

So, I packed up my stuff, lifted my rucksack up onto my back, and then walked into town. There was a bit of a spring in my step, a thrill, and a sense of satisfaction at having survived what proved to be a somewhat unexpectedly challenging, yet ultimately rewarding night. As I made my way up the street, I spotted some people who I'd ignored the day before. One of them called out to me again.

"Hey, Englais!" he shouted. "Do I make you angry? Why you run away when I call to you yesterday? I sorry."

This time I didn't ignore him and, since I was feeling in a much better mood, I walked over for a chat. It was Hairy camel-toes, and he was right, I was guilty as charged. I apologised for my previous rudeness.

It has taken me a few days to realise that Moroccans are just friendly people. They want our money, but that's just the game. They also want to know who we are and for all the best reasons. I wonder what I'm afraid of, and I don't have a suitable answer, just afraid of people maybe. Like many of my British counterparts, we are so used to being unfriendly to one another, and suspicious of everyone and everything foreign, that it comes as a shock when strangers want to know our business without also wanting to rob us, rape us, or blow us up for past crimes. After spending some time with him to make up for my previous ignorance, I continued on my way to get breakfast in a café. Then, after a splendid feast and catching up on my notes, it was time for me to do what I'd come to do - to head out into the desert alone.

Trekking Out

I leave Zagora on foot at 11 am after doing the one thing I swore would never happen; buying a carpet. It's made of wool and should help tonight when sleeping in the hammock. It cost me one hundred dirham, and they probably conned me, but I haggled him down from eight hundred and we both felt satisfied with the result. The carpet isn't full size, since only my back needs to be insulated. The rest of me can cope with that persistent breeze if it comes for me again tonight. It's light enough to carry, but it adds some awkwardness to my pack because of its thickness and shape. I also bought two litres of bottled water, and that's added a lot more weight to my pack. It's a noticeable burden to me now, as I head out of town.

I follow the main road for about half a mile to the edge of town, going back towards Ouarzazate. Just before reaching the end, I turn right and head into the back-alleys, hoping to make my way towards the River Draa. I switch my watch pedometer on, and I check my compass to note that I am heading East. I shouldn't need a compass, but think it's a good habit to get into. Before long, I reach the Palmerie. It's a criss-cross of dry, flat areas that appear to have been designed as farming spaces for growing food. Each area is a decent size and surrounded by mounds of earth that I can walk over. It's dense with palm trees, hence the name, and there is plenty of shade. Small earth huts serve as stores, and they fit in with the colour and texture of the ground they spring from, no doubt built in situ from the earth and by hand. The palms block the view from one square plantation to the next.

I make my way through a fair stretch of this, and I am nearly out the other side when I spot what I think is the river, or *was* the river. It's a wide expanse of flat river rocks, but there is no water. A river has carved it out at some point, but there's no sign of any water now. This is the edge of the Palmerie, and it is the start of the rocky desert. There will be no shade from here on. I'm feeling faint from the weight of the rucksack and despite the shade so far, the heat of the day is intensifying. Considering the situation, it makes me concerned. Some of my nervousness is because of the lack of knowledge regards camping in deserts. I also don't know where I'm headed, or what I'll find when I get there. For now, I conclude that I'm being overly sensitive to my well-being, but I will keep making mental checks on my situation.

A quick walk up and down the river's edge confirms it's devoid of water. I can't tell how long it's been dry. It could be a few days, or it could be years. Pulling up in the shade for a while, I pick a nearby palm tree to plonk myself down. I need to catch my breath and resuscitate, and I need to re-calibrate my plan. I'd expected to discover fresh flowing water here. It's also time to put on the headgear and prepare for the heat to increase as the day continues. Taking out the small piece of cloth they sold me back at Zagora, I try to turn it into a turban; it is when I discover just how small it is. At this point, I consider how important it is that I don't make any stupid mistakes.

I am careful to place my rucksack down in such a way that it doesn't invite scorpions to get beneath it, or worse, to climb up onto my straps. The heat is belting, and my focus is not where it should be. My confidence is not as bold as it was when I left. Remaining for a time against the palm tree, I relax to regain my composure. I'm feeling frustrated and need to get that in check.

Where I'm positioned, I can look out over the desert and have a one-eighty degree view. I scan it for both movement and potential camping spots. The mountains are still far off, beyond a long stretch of flat, rocky landscape that could be many miles distance. I'm no longer considering trying to reach them. Too much has changed and it would be foolish to try.

I spot two trucks in the distance to the north. They cross back and forth over the flat riverbed maybe a mile further up. I see some workers there too, they seem to be digging away at the rock with picks. Moroccans are far more acclimatised to this heat than I am, and they are bearing the full brunt of the hot midday sun out there. Flies bother my face, which suggests that I should be near water, but there isn't any I can find. I conclude it must be a water source in the Palmerie that I've just passed through. There must be some kind of irrigation system there, though I saw none.

I am surprised by a man appearing on a bicycle. He's following what I can now see is a rough dirt track that runs along the edge of the bank. Coming from the direction of the worksite to the north, he looks like he may have been doing a shift there. He stops when he gets near me. I can see his features are black African, not Berber or Moroccan. I ask him where the river has gone, and he understands enough to tell me it's empty, but adds nothing more. His features don't give away any expression, and I'm not sure if I should be wary of him. I remain relaxed to avoid signalling my uncertainty. He stares at me and then my rucksack, and I have the annoying feeling that he is weighing me up. I think about where my knife is, but it's packed too deep to reach, and isn't the best thing to be going for. To diffuse the discomfort, I talk more instead. I tell him there is a river in my guidebook and try to think about what else I can ask him, but he doesn't seem interested in talking further, or maybe just doesn't understand. A moment or two later, he gets back onto his bicycle and continues on his way along the bank path. He leaves giving no further acknowledgement or goodbye, and I breathe a sigh of relief. It wasn't a comforting interaction.

I'm confused by the lack of a river. It has thrown me out. I had noticed one on the way into town when I had first arrived in Zagora by taxi, and it had been gushing with water, so where is it? According to my *Lonely Planet Guide Book* map there should be a river here, and one with water in it. It shows up as blue in the book, but this one is definitely as dry as a bone. I scope the horizon, looking for clues as to where it's gone. I can make nothing out that hints at water being there. Its just dry rock everywhere out beyond the Palmerie. The stranger on the bicycle has given me reason to be nervous, and so I decide not to rest there any longer. It is time to cross the flats, aiming at a distant mound that I can see beyond the main riverbed with a palm tree that will offer some shade, and from there I'll decide on what to do next.

By the time I get across the riverbed, I am worn out from the exertion. The heat, along with the weight of the pack, has put me in danger of passing out under the scorching sun.

Amazed by how difficult such a simple task has become, I feel annoyed and ashamed at myself for not realising it would do this to me once the rucksack became badly weighted. I make a mental note: the next time I make a move it needs to be judged better and have some proper shade at the destination.

I had hoped that I would find signs of the river here, but there's nothing but hot rocks. Before I started across, I'd seen what looked like a channel where I hoped to find water, but it has turned out to be a deep and dry gully that borders the edge of the river bed on this side. It now thwarts my attempts to get across to the next part of the desert beyond.

I follow it for a way until I find a cutting that goes down into the channel itself, the sides are too steep to clamber up or down anywhere else. Climbing down the steep entryway, I then walk along inside the gully for a way, before finding another cut-out on the other side that allows me up and out.

Turning around, I make a mental note of what I am seeing, checking for prominent features to find the entry points again. I will need to know where they are, so on my return, I can aim at them. I also consider that it will look very different under the moon or by torchlight. If I have to leave at night, it will be challenging to get back across. The deep gully is an unexpected obstacle that creates additional concern for my return to safety. There is no other way to cross back except by taking the cut-outs. It's an empty moat with sheer sides blocking me from the relative safety of the town should I need it, and I'm aware of the increased risk to my situation because of it. I guess this is what the workers are doing out here. I still don't understand where the river has gone, but they must have redirected it, or are in the process of that, and maybe the gully has something to do with it. A lone palm tree marks the point of the channel exit where I stand,

and I am taking shade beneath it. I have to think in terms of one-hundred-metre distances now, dictated by my limited movement and my increased need for shade. I'm only three or four miles out from Zagora, and yet already I'm in a risky situation should anything go wrong here. If I fell over in a faint, no one might find me for days, weeks, maybe months. There are no obvious tracks on this side of the river bed, and no workers nor much else.

I err on the side of caution and decide that it's best to find a suitable spot to camp somewhere near where I am. It no longer makes sense to aim for those distant mountains, and though I am frustrated about that, I am now accepting of it too. The lack of flowing water has put me off making the extended trip. Also, knowing that retreat will be more difficult than originally planned, adds to the decision not to go too much further. My water supply won't last the trip from here to the mountains, but I've also not let anyone know where I'm headed, other than a waiter I befriended at breakfast, but he won't be alarmed if I never show up again.

I am feeling disappointed, and it's a tough pill to swallow. I'd had higher expectations. Mistakes like this are annoying, but it's also about sensible decision-making, and being aware of the dangers and limitations, *and* knowing when to accept them. Given the effect the heat is having on me and my wish to enjoy the trek and not suffer for it, I'll play safe. So, I decide to keep within whistling distance of the places that humans might pass by in a pinch. A loud wolf-whistle from where I am, might just reach across the expanse of the dry riverbed. Assuming someone was going by on that distant riverbank track, they should be able to hear me. The man on the bicycle has confirmed it is still in use, but now I have an additional concern. I noticed day-old tracks while I was down in the gully, made by a dog or something like it, but the size and gait of the tracks increased my concern for what I might face out here at night, as it wasn't a small animal. Rabies and wild dogs are a problem in Morocco, and I heard enough of them howling last night to assume packs of them are roaming around.

I clamber up a nearby incline to get a better view of my surroundings, then take some time to shade beneath another palm tree I find there. Despite its small size, I'm glad of the short piece of turban cloth that's protecting my head from the harsh sun. I drink some more water, keeping well hydrated will be the most important thing now. I'd planned to walk until about 4 pm and then set up camp wherever I got to, thus giving me about two hours before sundown to get situated. But that plan will now have to change, the heat has me beat. While in the palm's shade, I write up my notes to take my mind off things for a bit. After that, I leave my rucksack where it is and go for a walk to look around and try to spot a good place for a camp. I am passing out when away from the shade, so I return and sit down for a while longer. I find it strange that I am feeling it so much worse than I was in the Sahara further south. I conclude I must be draining my energy faster than I am used to, or aware of, and I need to keep conscious of that.

Again, I see the men working further up the riverbed, still over a mile away. From here, they look like small dots, but I can make out that they're working with hammers and picks in the same heat that is knocking me out. A dragonfly whizzes about me doing circuits and then darts off. Some birds land in the palm tree above my head and chatter for a while. I'm baffled by the flies and birds, since I can find no water at all to explain their presence. If there are insects, water should be less than a few hundred feet away.

It's 2 pm. I'm now sitting on a large raised area of rocks, trying to figure out how long ago this river flowed. It's carved out a wide channel at some point, so it must have been strong, and maybe six to ten feet deep, judging by the banks. Some areas near me seem to have had water irrigation channels feeding them and were maybe for growing stuff, but they don't look to be in use now. I wonder if the river got diverted, or if it's seasonal. I just don't know, and can't think what clues might give it away. Without knowing for certain, I have to consider that it may be a flood river. It could be a run-off from the distant mountains when it rains there, and that presents another kind of risk. So, I need to camp above it to avoid the risk of a flash flood if one comes during the night.

I have sat here now for over an hour. No one is around and I can find no signs of wells, boreholes, or a water source of any kind, and yet there are plenty of insects, birds, and even some scrub bushes, along with a scatter of random palm trees dotted about. Recovering my composure enough, I decide to head to another set of nearby palm trees to see if they will make a suitable spot to camp up.

Setting Up Camp

After picking a camp spot, I spend the next hour gathering firewood. It's tiring work and the only thing to be found is palm fronds. I'm not sure they will burn well, or for long, but there is nothing else around to use. I hope to gather enough for at least a cooking session. My most recent concern is that I've now spotted cat tracks that are about the size of my palm. I assume it's a lynx, or hope it is, but don't know, and I am camped right on top of one of its trails. It might not be too happy about that. Comfortingly, I have also just seen a ragged looking domestic cat, which I assume to be feral since there are no houses around here. With any luck, it won't just be me that is a potential dinner for a pack of dogs tonight.

Having seen no one out here the entire time, it surprises me to see a boy going past on a mule and cart some distance away towards the mountains in the east. He is following a track that I was not aware of behind my camp spot, and I think he saw me before I could sneak out of sight. There must be an adult with him somewhere, but I've seen no one else. I'm not sure if I am trespassing, but he seems to have stopped. To take my mind off the feeling that I shouldn't be there, I take comfort knowing that if I get bitten by something feral or feline tonight, I can assume someone will come by on the track within a day. I continue on with my firewood collecting as if nothing is untoward and soon hear a male voice to my right a little way off. I look up but can't see anyone, and then I hear the voice again. It can't be the boy, it's too deep in tone. It sounds as if he's talking to himself and then I catch movement out of the corner of my eye and spy a man walking around, who also appears to be collecting palm fronds some distance away. I've been careful to collect only old fallen ones and fronds that appear decaying. They might use palm fronds for their livelihood, for all I know, and the last thing I need is for someone to feel I'm robbing them. I don't think the man has seen me yet, and is moving gradually back towards where the boy was with the mule and cart. I want to turn around and look as he passes behind me, but I resist doing so. The boy then calls to him, and I assume he's pointing me out as a long silence follows. I continue fighting the urge to turn and look, but have the feeling he's coming over. So much for my khaki trousers making me invisible in the desert. Just as I'm hoping that I have got away without being spotted, I hear feet in the dirt behind me, and then stop. I stand up from my collection duty, and turn around, wondering what will transpire in the next few moments.

He's friendly enough, and I'm as polite as I can be. I don't understand his lingo and he doesn't understand mine. Maybe he's speaking Arabic or French. It's hard to discern, but I don't catch a single word of whatever he is trying to say to me. I tell him I'm there to write about the birds and the animals - which is bullshit, of course - but I think after a while and some hand motion he sort of gets it. He nods sagely before looking at my pile of palm fronds. Ah, awkward moment. I ask if it's his land, and I'm now using lots of arm gestures to impart my meaning. Again, he seems to respond in the affirmative, but it's not all that clear that he understands. He doesn't seem bothered about my being there, otherwise I assume he would have tried to make me leave, which he has not suggested. The fact he isn't shooing me away I take to be a good sign, but the way he watches me is giving me the impression he hasn't fully decided what's going on yet. It's hard to know where all this is going to end up, and the ball is in his court. I can't figure him out, and he can't figure me out either. I guess it must look pretty odd to a Moroccan. He's more than happy to just stand there and watch me - they seem to do that a lot. Is he the landowner, or is he no one? He's not that old, maybe in his late twenties or thirties. He must know that I plan to spend the night there. Even though I haven't yet set my hammock up, the rucksack is a give-away for my intentions. That and the recent dugout fireplace with a collection of palm fronds laying beside it. For want of something else to resolve our communication difficulties, I point to the cat tracks and then make a sound as if to be enquiring about them. I hope this builds on my attempts to appear as an amateur photographer or budding David Attenborough. He looks at the tracks, then points to the feral cat that's now stalking something beside a small bush. I don't see how a cat that size can make human-sized paw prints, but when I make out like it's some large ferocious beast, he laughs and says, "Non."

A long silence ensues. I have run out of anything else to talk to him about, not that he understood anything I said, anyway. He remains standing there, motionless, watching me. I can't offer him tea, or else I might have done. Now feeling awkward and not sure what to do or say next, I produce a packet of cigarettes and offer him one, but he refuses. Taking one out, I light up nervously. I'm at a loss to know what we are supposed to do next in this situation, but after a moment longer just staring at me, he then pats his right arm to his chest and extends his hand out towards me in one motion, as if to say goodbye. I react from a place of intense nervousness and involuntarily step forward, putting a hand out for a shake in return. He seems bemused by this gesture, and I realise he may not have ever met a westerner before. He looks at my hand for a moment and then cautiously gives me his in return and we engage in a limp, "wet-fish" handshake. I forget they don't do handshakes in Muslim countries. Oops. After this final, awkward experience, he then departs, and I am left wondering if a gaggle of inquisitive Moroccans will come by after he gets where he's going. Or worse, those scary looking police.

Having now been discovered, I no longer feel the need to lurk about, which takes a weight off my mind. My presence here has now been endorsed, since he didn't run me off. I sit down to take a break and watch a dust devil tear down the wide, empty flats of the dry riverbed. I am on a ledge about twenty feet up above its floor. It's a good vantage point, and my position faces west. The dust devil moves like an angry spirit in search of something, and it passes across the entire length of the empty river before running out of energy. It's outstanding to see it throwing up dust hundreds of feet into the air from the spinning cone.

The man, the boy, and their mule have gone off towards the south, and soon after, a pleasant silence descends. I look at my collection of palm fronds and decide that I need to spend another hour foraging. I need enough burning material to last the night, should I require it. It's 4 pm, but I want to wait until I'm sure that I am alone rather than be caught making further excursions too far out over this territory. It is hard to know if I am on public land or someone's property. He never gave me a conclusive answer, and neither do I know whether using palm fronds is okay or considered theft.

There are many more flies out in the afternoon, and they are taking a liking to me. As the sun drops, the day finally cools, and I wonder what other beasties are planning to appear. The night will bring out the hunters, and I'm not well enough versed in what might be around, or how big they might get.

So far I have drunk a little over half a litre of water and eaten one energy bar about two hours ago. The bite to eat sorted me out from the heady spins I was having.

[I didn't know this at the time of writing, but when I returned to England and revisited my trip notes, I learnt it was far less water than I should have been drinking in that heat. I should have been taking extra salt, too. When I discovered this later, it went a long way to explain my dizzy spells that day.]

I have one energy bar left, a tin of sardines, and some tuna. If I can get a fire going, then I can have some spaghetti too, assuming I have enough water. The plan to use river water for cooking didn't turn out as expected.

Some kids are playing in a green patch some distance away on the other side of the river bed near the Palmerie. They are down at the edge of the flats a little way to the north, probably about half a mile up on the other side. They haven't seen me, and I want to keep it that way, as kids will always be inquisitive. I wonder what time everyone goes home for supper around here.

After collecting some more palm fronds, I decide that it's time for my last energy bar. They were a fine investment, and it gets me through. I'll have to leave it until as late as possible to put up the hammock, as I don't want anyone else wandering by to be drawn to want to investigate. I especially do not want those kids seeing it. It's bound to make them curious and want to visit if they spot me or the hammock. I'm surprised at just how many people have been around. It's nothing but desert for miles and I am four miles out from Zagora, according to my watch pedometer. I guess people will go as far as necessary to work on the land. I probably shouldn't be concerned. Does anyone care about a white guy camped up in their desert? It's just rocks and a few palm trees.

Seeing the hardship that people work and live under out here brings about a sense of guilt. It is hard to swallow or appease. Morocco is an excellent introduction to that side of Africa. I am a foreigner out of place, a rich white tourist to them, and I think I present an opportunity. It's an awareness which makes me nervous because I only have to meet one bad-ass, and I'll have trouble. White folk are privileged and rich by design, or so we are told. Though I'm not convinced this is really the case, I can see why it's seen that way when we can afford to travel around the world and enjoy the lifestyle we do. It makes me nervous while out here. I do not fit in and get noticed easily, and knowing *that* puts me on edge. I have learnt from my years in London to expect trouble from strangers. Living in a big city, now and then you will inevitably get challenged by someone. It's my experience in life that you will often be targeted, not because of who you are, but because of what you represent to another person. It is often opportunistic. And being white or European, and travelling alone, is enough to put me in that box. The more I think about the African on the bike I met earlier in the day, the more I consider he was checking out my bag, while the guy collecting palm fronds was merely curious about what I was doing there.

So, is being white really a privilege? Certainly not in a Grand Taxi. Sometimes I think it just makes us an obvious target, but I suppose it is a privilege in some situations. Many white people seem to think of themselves as superior, but then I find most people think little of other cultures that are not their own. I can't pretend that I am *not* better off than the people I am seeing out here, monetarily speaking. I make more money, and I have an easier work-life. Okay. But then I am still broke, I have no home of my own, and am miserable if I am honest about it. Is "cash value" the only way we measure people in this equation? It seems to be. But issues are always relative, and my world would present some serious challenges to someone from Morocco, most especially the cost of survival there. I have known indigenous people who would laugh at the idea that white people are better off. They think Westerners, Europeans, and Americans, especially, are the ones in a state of crisis. And they have a point. We are often angry, drugged up, emotionally confused, rootless, homicidal, and suicidal maniacs. So, I agree with the indigenous viewpoint to some extent. I think white people stew in a trained, ingrained sense of guilt, a disconnection from family roots and their ancestors, and living this way is something that we have been taught us to assume is real and founded, and worse, superior. What if it isn't? We consider white people to be the root of colonialism and Empire, the cause of slavery, and the perpetrators of economic abuse. It is very easy to see it that way on the surface, but is that really what has been going on? Whites have also helped to make the world a better place and led the way in technological, medicinal, as well as a multitude of other advances. So why is everything now conveniently the fault of white people?

That kind of messaging has been in our culture for decades, but doesn't stand up well to proper questioning. I blame the Charity sector for creating the message, endorsing it, driving it, and lying about it too, because it makes those same white people part with money. White guilt funds the World Bank and IMF. Whites will happily part with cash to appease their ingrained and taught sense of guilt. And yet we rarely ever question that relationship. White people have been throwing cash at the World Bank since 1940s, and yet nothing has been fixed in Africa, so what gives? At what point will reparations be enough? Trillions of dollars pumped into Africa and to achieve what? I think charity is just another form of colonialism. What makes a white European assume a black African needs our help anyway? We think we have a better life, but white people can be miserable creatures. Yet this is the message they have hammered into us from a young age with - *"think of the poor starving Ethiopians"* . But this is a slogan, do you live a better life than the average African? I know plenty of miserable and broke white people. I never figured out the truth of this equation, and most white people never question it, because they *fear* questioning it. So, we accept the accusation and take the blame at face value. No one would dare suggest it might be untrue.

I don't buy into that narrative, but being out here and seeing how many Moroccans live has left me feeling pangs of guilt based on my skin colour and sense of privilege. If that's genuine or just because of my upbringing as a white person, I don't know. All I can do is be humbled by what I find here, and feel grateful for what I get to experience in coming to these places. Being respectful is a good start, but I need a certain amount of self-preservation to get by too. I've made the choice to travel to Morocco and then wander out into their desert and spend a few nights in solitude here. I will, in a few days, return to my mind-numbing existence as a privileged white man working all the hours available in the city of London to pay for my existence in that world. The privilege, if there is one, is in the ability for me to do that. The human condition is a peculiar thing. How can we compare one life to another and balance it off equally? But then, isn't that exactly what a privileged person would say?

It's 4:30 pm and those kids aren't making signs of packing up and going home yet. I am right in their line of vision if they look up long enough to notice. The flies are being a real pain now, and I can also feel a sunburn developing on my face. *Oh, you stupid Brit!* I didn't put on sun-screen because somewhere in my mind I thought I would get a tan that way and the headscarf would protect me enough not to need it. Figuring that the desert and the last few days might have been enough to give me a base-layer, turns out I was wrong. Sometimes I get away with it, but not this time. I check my reflection in my stainless steel cooking pot and see that my face is beetroot red. I don't feel too bad, but I won't know until the sun goes down and the tingles come on.

Somewhere behind me on the track, I hear voices again, but can't see anyone. All I wanted was to find some peace to relax in. Morocco, it seems, isn't the best place to come for that. Even four miles out into the desert, and people are going by.

It's about one hour until sundown and the night will be a whole other issue to contend with. I'm not sure what else I can prepare while I wait for darkness to fall and for those kids to leave. Given my easily spotted location on this raised rocky area, I'm feeling cautious. Two sets of people have gone by on the donkey track behind my camp that I didn't even know was there, though it could have been the same man and boy again. I wouldn't say my wild-camping is going perfectly to plan yet.

The worst aspect is my paranoia about having to deal with people. I just can't seem to relax around other human beings, especially foreign ones. It's too late to move on or turn back now. I'm in this spot for the night, like it or not. I want to relax and enjoy it, and I also want to get my hammock set up before dark. While the ever-present risk of attracting more unwanted attention looms, I can't risk putting the hammock up or lighting the fire, they will see it too easily from the track and those kids playing over the other side of the river bed would see it too. My camp fire is prepped and ready to go, and I am half-unpacked and ready to put up the hammock as soon as those kids leave, but that is now looking like it won't happen until the sun fully sets, which means a rush job for me once it does.

I'm having conflicting emotions. As I sit here with nothing else to do but wait, I wonder if I might be crazy. I mean, fully crazy, and not just a bit loose in the head. Who does stuff like this? If it weren't for my recent discovery of Ray Mears and his Bushcraft TV show, I wouldn't have had the guts to be doing this at all. Traditionally, this kind of behaviour has been the domain of the S.A.S. or Rambo nut-jobs who were best avoided. Ray's show made me realise that wasn't the case, and that it was okay to want to camp outside in the wilds. It was something I always felt drawn to do, but I kept quiet about that. I used to feel like I might be nuts for thinking about it, so I rarely saw it through. I didn't want to be thought of as the loner Rambo type. Ray was the first to make me realise it was more than just a psychotic survivalists wet-dream, and that it was also the domain of people who loved nature, being in nature, and the wilds. He made me see it wasn't just for the loners and nut jobs, and in discovering that, I felt a tremendous relief. Many of us live in hermetically sealed bubbles of existence. On a normal day, I don't even know what the weather is doing, as I spend most of my time in air-conditioned offices or centrally heated houses with double glazing. The Rambo connotation put me off camping out in the wild. I had risked it once or twice, but had no proper education in it, and didn't know what I was doing. I still don't, but I am learning now. Before Ray Mears, I had only ever come across the Rambo types of people, and it had put me off. But now, finally, with those TV shows entering the mainstream and becoming more acceptable to the masses, the perception is changing. Ray Mears is making it acceptable to the average person. So, it's thanks to Ray that I am out here. Thanks Ray! I remind myself of that now, but to be honest, it doesn't help in dealing with the situation at hand, and I still feel insane for being out here.

Finishing up my notes, I decide that if those kids haven't budged by the time I finish my next smoke, then just out of a need to be more comfortable and enjoy the sunset, I am going to set up the hammock and light my fire, regardless. I don't know why I am being so twitchy about it all. I just don't want to deal with strangers in the desert. But it's time to stop being such a goose about the whole thing and just get on with it. So, I finish my smoke and then set about the task.

I get the hammock up between two palm trees, but soon discover they are slightly too close together. There is only about eight feet between them and it's not ideal. Another couple of feet would have been a lot better. But with a rush for time before it gets dark, and with no better set of trees near where I am located, it will have to do. This means the hang of the hammock isn't as taut as it should be, and sags down near to the ground when I get in to test it. I also notice that the occasional breeze lifts the covering tarp up, enough that, if it should rain heavily, it's likely to hit the hammock cocoon beneath and get me wet. That's a worry, and so I spend the next period adjusting it as best I can. Adding enough tension to stretch the overhanging tarp and it should protect me better. It's the consideration of rain, or an unexpected flash flood from the distant mountains, that now makes me assess my choice of location. It shouldn't rain, but if it rains, one has to assume it will be a deluge, and that's why I chose the upper ground. Though it makes me more visible, I'm best placed for that kind of event by being as high up as I can get. It stands as the right choice, given all the relevant scenarios I could predict. With the lowering light, I sort through my items so I can find them all after dark.

Carpet, *check*.
Empty rucksack, *check*.
Sleeping bag, money-bag, spare torch, *check*.
What I need in the hammock, *check*.
And what I need nearby, *check*.
Warm clothes and a woolly hat go on, *check*.
And then I put my head-torch on and test it, *check*.

I still have some daylight left, but I won't by the time I am done setting up. Unnecessary items I hang above "dog height" on the convenient natural hooks that I find growing on the palm tree trunk. I place them under the leaning side of the trunk to keep them dry if that deluge I am not expecting should come. My fire-starting kit, food, and water are down beside the roughly dug out fire pit. The pit is a shallow area I dug out to protect it against blustery wind and to hide the light of the flames, so it won't be seen so easily across the dry riverbed.

I think and rethink what I will need tonight and the process slows me down a bit, not to mention my brain slips easily into daydreams after the rigours of the day. It's been far more tiring than I had expected it to be. There have been very few moments of relaxation, nor much pleasure, not right now at least. It's been hectic, tense, often painfully so, and far too hot to be comfortable, but then maybe that's why it's called *"survival"*. Der. Maybe the benefit comes from making it home in one piece and feeling like you handled a challenge to the senses, or didn't, but at least it's over. Maybe with practice and familiarity - and with more first-hand knowledge - I will feel different from how I do right now. Currently, I feel like I am only just getting away with it. Once again, I am feeling far from confident, and instead feel incapable and a little ashamed at not being better than I am. Self-worth can be such a bitch.

I'm all set up by 7 pm, and I ignite the fire just as the light beings to fade against the day. Missing out on enjoying the sunset because I was too busy wrestling with hammock issues, but things feel set and in place now. My body aches, and I can feel the dry burn from too much sun on my skin. It isn't pleasant, but the fire lights with surprising ease, and as it gets going, I discover palm fronds are perfect for tinder, kindling, and medium-long burn time. They are the ideal fire ingredient. Smoky at first, but quickly losing their initial flame and then turning to a good ember that lasts for a while. Fantastic! I realise I have more than enough fire material for the night, and I can afford to be quite liberal with it, though I won't be leaving a fire burning when I get into the hammock just in case a wind picks up. I can't imagine it would be easy to set fire to anything out here in this desert, but I don't want to discover that it is. It's perfectly calm out here now, much less wind than last night, and for that I am grateful. With the darkness falling, the flies have also disappeared, and no mosquitoes so far, either. Woo-hoo! I've been quite lucky in that respect because those little vampires love my sweet, white privileged blood.

I burn the cigarette butts that I have smoked, and I keep a check not to drop any rubbish. I decide I'm not all that hungry and can't be hassled with making spaghetti, especially if it's going to use up all my water. So I opt instead for making a cup of tea. The flat fronds make a good ledge to sit the pot on, and it soon boils. The tea is great and having a warmed belly is incredibly comforting. I then devour the sardines, and realise how hungry I was, but they are enough, and so I decide to save the tin of tuna for breakfast.

I sit and stoke the fire with palm fronds, feeding it and staring into it as I do. The darkness of night soon falling around me, and the half-moon has grown larger than it was yesterday. It rises from the east to turn the landscape into a bright, white, silvery-blue that becomes a fascinating feature to be immersed in. It all looks so completely alien, and I am now a part of it. Rather than the reddish Mars landscape of the Sahara, it feels like I could be on the Moon this time, or maybe Mercury. With no breeze at all and very little noise, I am finally alone in the wilds. I stand up and stare into the peculiar world that exists in the moonlight landscape all around me in every direction. The concerns of the day are gone, and I feel like I am in some kind of magic time. Everything looks so completely different now. Too tired to even think or focus, I am merging into it, becoming a part of it, even I am now the same silvery-blue monochrome. My journey to reach this moment is over. Here I am. I have arrived. This, the moment I came looking for. And with neither the energy left to wonder about it, nor to ponder the effort it took to get to this place, there is nothing of me left to give and I stand in a day dream staring at it all. Stripped bare of any emotion or worry, I become a part of the night-time landscape and soon disappear into the moonlit, milky silence.

In The Land Of The Silvery Blue

I don't know what I got up to after dark. I recall being part of a mesmerising silvery blue and wandering around looking at the shadows and the shapes that were unique to that world. Tired beyond my rational limits, neither fear nor wonder seemed to register. I was just there, a part of it, and lost in it. What I remember most was a sense of calm and a feeling of wholesomeness. There was an awareness that I liked the sense of being out of my normal state. I was alone on the moon, and it felt wonderful.

At some point I returned to my hammock, opened up the zipper, leaned back into the sling, and then threw my legs up and over and then wiggled down into position. The moment that I got into the hammock, it was like returning to a spaceship, and everything became familiar once again. Inside, still under the bright moonlight, I could make out my sleeping bag and wrestled to get it into place around me. It was a struggle to get into it from within the confines, and I was swinging around in the air for a while. But once done, I felt toasty and content. I lay there for a long time smiling and happy, but still too charged to fall asleep.

Then the bark of a distant dog broke the spell. Its intermittent yelps cutting through the night that had been humming all around me until then. I listened to its sound, unconcerned at first, but as it got closer, my mind latched onto to the developing sense of danger that it might present. Soon, it was close enough to be a worry. And as it grew more audible, so it became the agitated howl of an animal that sounded like it was in distress. The sound was not a healthy, happy one, and at that point I wondered if it was rabid, and immediately fear gripped me. My hammock was far too low to the ground, and made of a thin mesh material, so there was nothing much to protect me from a mad dog. During the day, I'd been worried about wild cats, but now I had something worse to worry about. Wild dogs would be harder to deal with. From the continued barking, it seemed to be headed my way, and I thought about what action I should take if it got close. I was armed with a decent knife, but against a rabid dog, the best course of action would be to scale a palm tree and wait it out. A cartoon image of the scene appeared in my mind and brought some relief.

Between the barks, all I could hear was my heartbeat hammering away in my chest. I was trying to measure the distance the dog was away from me as it telegraphed its movements and position. My last resort would have to be the palm tree, as I could not imagine stabbing a dog to death without getting bitten. I was feeling exhausted after the long day, and a part of me felt like going to sleep and pretending that none of it was happening, but the drawn-out periods of silence just increased my uncertainty and discomfort. If I fell into sleep, the next moment would be followed by a growl, a snarl, or howl that would pull me back into a disorientated and adrenalin-fuelled wakefulness. It was the last thing I needed to be going through. The dog edged closer. Until it seemed to stop only a few hundred yards away, and there it stayed, barking for another thirty minutes.

As I continued to listen, and tried to ascertain its distance and state, a new thought occurred to me; that maybe it wasn't rabid, but had got stuck in the deep gully. I got images of a lost mutt and the more I considered it, the more it seemed like a plausible explanation. It was also the one I wanted to believe in. The barking diminished in intensity and was becoming less aggressive, but it was still close, and it occurred often enough that sleep would not be forthcoming until something was done. Against my better judgement, but out of a need for unbroken sleep, I thought about either rescuing it or just encouraging it to move on. By now, I was so annoyed and tired of the situation that the initial fear became a non-issue. I just wanted to get some sleep. It also created a good excuse to get back out into that alien landscape. After a few more times being jarred awake, I could take it no more, and decided that it was time to deal with the hound.

When I left the hammock, the same thing happened, and I lost all track of time. All the fear, concern, and even the desire for sleep, were gone once I was out there. I think that my memory had no point of reference from which to store the experience, and my senses didn't function as they normally would, so I became lost in the land of the silvery moonlight. I don't know how long I was gone for, nor what I did. Just that I left planet earth and went walking in an hallucination. I didn't find the dog, I don't recall even looking for it. As far as I can remember, I heard no further barking once I left the hammock. I have no recollection of events, other than to know that I liked the feeling of being out there immensely. It was like an elevated dreaminess that had no emotional content attached, as if I didn't exist as anything more than a ghost, and to be that way was a relief. I was grateful to the hound for giving me a reason to get out of the hammock again. When I returned from my second visit into that strange silvery world, I fell asleep quickly, and I don't recall hearing the howling again that night, but that was where the fun ended for other reasons.

Why They Call It "Survival"

I woke on the hour, every hour, from 1 am to 6 am. I was freezing each time. It was one hell of a night. The wool carpet kept my back warm, but that imperceptible ice-cold breeze was back, and it found its way in everywhere it could. Whatever part of my body it got to sent a chill to my core. Any warmth it left me with I focused on to stay sane. I considered lighting the fire, but being tired and cold also put me off the idea. It felt safer in the hammock than out of it. I wouldn't have slept on the ground even with a fire, and if the mad dog was to come by, rabies was a worse risk than being cold for a night. It may have been illusory, but I felt more protected in the hammock. I knew that I just had to make it to the morning, but I wanted desperately to sleep. Each hour that I woke up, I made a simple assessment of my situation and my question was this - *"Can I survive this until morning?"* And each time the answer was *"yes"*, despite it being unpleasant. So I just kept repeating a mantra to myself - *"I will get over this tomorrow. Tonight, all I have to do is survive."*

It's a funny thing, knowing that you are in a bad way

while also knowing exactly what reserves you have to recover at the end of the ordeal. Had there been wind or rain in the night, I'd have been in more serious trouble and would have had to act accordingly. I was semi-delirious as it was, but that was because I was so worn out from the day's shenanigans, I could barely move to fight it. So, I sunk into a place inside myself and camped out there instead. I observed my suffering from that vantage point, and from there I counted down the time to my escape.

When I considered this event later, it was a risky thing to do. I could sense the point at which I could fade out. It began with a sensation that felt like sleep, and though it was *not* sleep, I knew where the line was. I wasn't that close to it, but I was on the way towards it. The discomfort was intense, and the cold pushed me there, and with it, that icy chill brought a sinister promise. It told me about a refuge from its suffering, I just had to give in to it, and it didn't seem all that hard to do. If a part of me had had enough of living, I could have drifted off towards that place easily. It was inviting me to leave in the same way that sleep invites you to escape the aches of the day; simply by letting go and falling towards it. In the days that followed, I considered this at length, and it was quite an eerie thing to be aware of.

I kept up the observation of my mental meanderings as I struggled to handle the cold. I knew how many hours I had left until dawn, and I knew that once the sun came up over the horizon, it would save me. If I then drank some water, ate my tin of tuna, and boiled up a cup of tea, I should recover quickly. Then, by about 8 am, it would be as if nothing had happened. I just had to survive the experience until then. While I bore through the time with a shiver, I determined to observe the event and its subtleties for future reference.

Such is the simple nature of our end. We can brush very

close to it daily, and we tend not to believe it when we do. It can breathe its cold, soporific, calmness upon us, and when it does so, we don't acknowledge that it is just a small step away. We can't grasp that. One mis-timed step into a busy street, or an absent thought as we drive through a red light. We have only to make the mistake once, and people do. We forget this in our day-to-day existence, believing instead that we are immortal beings, but we aren't, and sometimes something reminds us of that truth. It was one of those times. Experiencing that kind of awakening was what I went out there to do. Whether I was consciously pushing myself at it, I am not sure. Though I think it was just where I was at in my life; it drew me to want to know, to feel the bite of life and death. I wanted to understand how far I could sink before I became lost or damned. I wanted to know what gauges I had, what to trust to advise me at that moment. How long could I survive out there, and how long would it take me to recover? In retrospect, I could see that I was testing myself, testing my limits, testing my body, and testing my forbearance to suffering. I was looking for the markers at the edge, to learn about them.

With no warmth and very little sleep, I passed the time thinking about the errors I had made and the lessons to be learned. I needed to understand the nature of the chill that was working on me and how to deal with it in the future. There was no doubting what it could do to me. It spoke to me about death. I was borderline delirious, though I felt certain that I knew how to escape the situation if it came to it. I was also sure I had enough strength to make it to morning, and so I let it nip at me. I wanted never to forget the experience. Willing to experience it *this* time, so that next time I would look for ways to avoid going through it again.

A simple tent or tarp construct would have helped much

more than a hammock did. I needed something to protect me from that subtle breeze, and a hammock on open land just let the thing right in. I was far too vulnerable to a lot of things in that hammock.

The night seemed to last forever. Each hour dragging on like a punishment that I had inflicted upon myself, and I questioned the point of my existence many times. When 6.30 am came around, shivering, distressed, tired, and embattled, I emerged from my cocoon into the growing ambient light. Those last moments spent waiting for the sun to rise over the mountains to the east felt like a purgatory spent before eternity. It was burning the experience so deep into my being that I felt certain I would tattoo it onto my bones. I wanted never to forget the sensation of being that close to the edge. Sure, I could have lit a fire, but some part of me chose not to. So, I shut my eyes and felt for the edge of oblivion, that place where the cold became something else. The wait for the sun was excruciating, and I was begging for it to rise over the mountains. And then it got to the point where I couldn't move my hands enough to light a fire even if wanted to.

The sun hit my face at 7 am, and I never felt so grateful to see it. The yellow rays breaking over the peaks of the distant mountains were like colour prisms that burst into the world and began throwing life-giving energy at me. They were weak at first, with barely any warmth at all. I began dancing around in them with my eyes still shut, like a savage trying to conjure heat from the gods to bring my body back some life.

By 7.30 am I was resuscitating, but I felt like absolute crap. I had been looking forward to the tuna, but hadn't checked the cheap tin opener, and it was at this point I discovered it was broken (the sardines had come with a roller that meant they didn't require a tin opener). Having no dexterity in my muscles or fingers, I didn't dare risk hurting myself further by attempting to burgle the tin with a rock or the knife. It was another lesson arrived at the hard way, and so there was nothing to eat. Hunger was going to make my four-mile trek back to civilisation that bit harder. I considered making a fire and the time it would take to get a cup of tea on the go, but there were other issues to consider now. I knew I had the cool of the morning, but it would soon turn the tables to the opposite problem - not one of cold, but heat. The cool I had now, would make walking safer and much easier than yesterday, but I needed to leave immediately if I was going to take advantage of that. I was warming up, but I was also worn out, and I knew that if I left it much longer, then I might pass out in the heat that would develop, and that would not be good.

So, I buried the camp fire from the evening before, then cleared the dirt around my site to make sure I left no trace of my being there. I distributed the remaining palm fronds about the place and made a point of returning it to how I had found it. Functioning also helped me warm me up a bit, and my mind came back to a sense of purpose by engaging in practical action, which felt good. I double-checked to make sure I was leaving nothing behind, and then took a moment to thank the palm trees for the shade, the dog for not biting me, the subtle breeze for not killing me, and the desert for an experience that I might eventually come to appreciate, if I could just get through the last challenges facing me. Then I threw my rucksack up onto my back and made my way towards the cut-out of the gully. I was aiming to return the same way I had come; across the ditch and the big dry riverbed, heading back towards Zagora where I would reward myself with strong coffee and a hearty breakfast.

Hotel Palmerie

I make Zagora a few hours later and eat at the first café that I find. The chill finally leaves my bones, and I start to feel more myself. Coffee and an omelette bring back some energy, and my mind focuses for the first time since I walked out into the hot, dry riverbed yesterday. I get a sense of just how way-out I was getting and commend myself for correctly recognising my state last night. I now conclude it is easy to find oneself in a life-threatening situation, and yet also to be oblivious to it. It could happen just one or two miles out of town and you wouldn't realise how close to trouble you were, and even deny it was happening. I am sure I came close to disaster at least twice yesterday, the biggest culprits being the heat and the cold. There seem to be two states of being; either you are making your way towards life-giving things, or away from them, and I was headed the wrong direction several times over the last twenty-four hours. The trick to dealing with it is to think ahead, have fall-back plans and strategies in place, rules and guidelines for any situation to divert you away from acting in ways that could drain you further.

After eating, I am still feeling a bit knocked out, but I am definitely on my way back to good health. What I need now is a day off to recover and enjoy all that I have achieved this trip. I check the guidebook and find a hotel with a pool available at the other end of Zagora. It looks to be exactly what I need, so I finish up my coffee and head out to find it.

I walk in to the Hotel Palmerie at the southern end of the main drag in Zagora. It has everything I need and offers acceptable, cheap rooms that have air-con and en suite showers. It's a pleasant respite for 100 dirham a night, so I book in and go to find my room. I get myself washed and shaved, then I wash my dust-covered t-shirt and khaki trousers in the sink and hang them to dry using the twisted elastic bungee rope I brought for the task. I then go through my pack and re-organise it. Finally, I am ready to get down to a bit of well-deserved rest and resuscitation, and I head down to the pool.

There seems to be no one else around. The hotel is empty. I wander through the premises and don't see a single person. Returning to the pool area, I get settled in. Sun-bathing the unbaked parts of my body seems like a good place to start. It's midday as I write this and I'm feeling good. A little dazed still from the experience, but that's to be expected. It took it out of me, but once I feel fully recovered, I'm sure it will hold gems of knowledge. It was hard work, and pretty worrying at moments, but I made it through. And now here I am, luxuriating beside a pool, the sun beaming down from a cloudless blue sky, no one to bother me, nothing to do, just chill by the water and feeling groovy. What a contrast to yesterday.

Our bodies have a natural ability to function towards a

state of recovery. It has always fascinated me that if we create the right conditions, we automatically get better. What a miraculous phenomenon. We are self-healing creatures. Most things deteriorate, erode in the atmosphere, but our bodies heal. It's like a magic trick. So long as we don't go beyond defined points of damage, then the recovery can happen quickly. You only have to provide it with a few things to achieve this process. One of those is an environment to relax in, and the other is allowing the mind to find a calm place. It's important to know I am safe, and no longer in a potentially hazardous situation. A stress-free situation.

What is also clear to me is that it is the practical and learnt knowledge that stops us making mistakes and pushing ourselves beyond our limits. It's not our instincts or messages from the body that save us from difficult situations. This isn't what I was expecting to discover, quite the opposite in fact, so I am surprised. I thought my body would tune in to an instinctive "knowing" of what to do while I was out there, but what is apparent to me in retrospect is that it is logical, known, and quantifiable measures that make or break a situation. I am not sure I will trust my instincts so readily again. When I return to London, I will research more about survival requirements and stick to the recommended thresholds. *Water, shelter, warmth, safety, energy, health.*

Another big takeaway from this trip is that our body has no real gauge for when we need water. I wasn't thirsty yesterday, and so I spent the entire time dehydrating contentedly. The only way to meet the correct water requirement is to drink a set amount based on environmental factors. It should be a calculated figure. This is something I didn't do at all, and will research into it further when I get home to establish what I should have done, and how much water I should have been drinking while in the desert. I didn't register that I was dehydrating, but on looking back now, I can recall that I was doing stupid and irrational things and spending half my time in a daze because of it. There were moments when I was just staring into space for long periods while lost in an overheating daydream. I should have been looking out for myself better and not sitting in the thirty-five-degree heat while trying to get a suntan in under a minute. I put most of my dizzy behaviour yesterday down to dehydration, and I need to avoid making that kind of mistake again.

The moment that we need to seek safety, or need help, our mind and body are usually in a state of confusion. When that happens, the signals it gives us are often wrong, misunderstood, or misleading. It's then that the rational mind, common-sense, and practical knowledge can step in and save us. Instinct can cloud good decision making in that kind of situation. Listening only to our bodily signals - or our instincts - in a difficult situation might make things worse.

Having just gone through a situation of extremes, I will seek to avoid doing it again in quite the same way in the future because there is no need to. That was another realisation from the experience; why have a survival situation when I can have a good time? Yesterday could have been much more enjoyable if I had not tortured myself. So why was I doing it? I was deliberately pushing my limits to feel first hand just where those limits were. In part, I was doing it to recognise those limits. I wanted to forensic and assess a difficult situation, just as I am doing now, and to discover from it how to better prepare myself for future trips into wild places. I needed to do it to know where my edges were and to feel what happens when they were close to being crossed. As I suspected might be the case, now that I am away from the desert and the adventure is over, I feel thrilled, euphoric, and invigorated. Yesterday, and in the early hours of this morning, I deliberately walked a knife-edge along a precipice that could have done damage if I had gotten too close to it. Last night felt close several times, especially around 5 or 6 am, because by then it was all getting too much. It's a genuine danger to make mistakes out there. Little ones can lead to big ones quickly, and trouble escalates rapidly. A simple choice, such as going looking for a barking dog in the night, could have had dire consequences if I had found the creature. I am still confused about exactly why I did that. I think I was just so tired that I couldn't take hearing the distress of its howling any longer and wanted to put us both out of its misery. But the list of dangers out there is endless. Some key things to think about now, that I suspect would be generic to most trips out into wild places, go as follows:

The heat, the cold, a lack of food, a lack of water, physical injury, poisoning, an unexpected sudden illness, incorrect assessment of a dangerous situation, the unknown and the unexpected that can never be predicted, being too far away from help or, conversely, being too close to humans that might not be friendly. If rain or dew had come last night, I would have been considerably worse off today. Then I might have failed to have a successful trip. Morale is one of the biggest challenges, even on relatively brief trips. The sense of failure can quickly lead to stupid decision-making and pushing limits too far. I learnt a lot from this excursion, and I made it out in one piece and uninjured. Fan-fucking-tastic!

The swimming pool is great. Though no one is around in

the hotel, it's still early, so maybe the other guests are in bed or have already gone out, assuming there are any. This afternoon, the sun should fall on the pool area perfectly, right until it dips behind the high walls that surround the hotel. I can see over them from here, and beyond is nothing but the flat and rocky desert. I am facing the opposite direction from where I trekked out yesterday.

I have taken the entire day off to rest up beside the water here for all of it. Do nothing but laze about, swim, sun my skin, and write up my notes. Tomorrow I'll belt back across the country to Ouarzazate, and then on to Marrakech by Grand Taxi, or a bus if I can find one. That trip will take all of Thursday, and then on Friday I plan to take the train from Marrakech to Casablanca, and on Saturday, I have to catch my flight home. I want to see some more of Morocco and if any of it appeals to me, maybe plan for future ventures.

I read a book on a shelf in the reception area here about a marathon called *Marathon des Sables*. They hold it in Morocco, close to where I am now. People run day and night through the desert with only what they can carry to sustain themselves. I am shocked by this. My petty trek out into the heat of the day, just four miles walk from Zagora, was nothing compared to what those crazy runners put themselves through. I am also surprised to read that they have had no deaths since the races began in 1986, and it's run yearly ever since. The closest incident was someone who got lost and turned up twelve days later. They had run four hundred kilometres off-course and were found in Algeria alive and well. Wow! It certainly put my little trek to shame. I feel somewhat humbled by reading it, maybe a little pathetic in comparison.

What the hell, it's all relative, and I never trained for this trip. This was my first solo desert experience, and I didn't understand until now just what I would be up against, nor just how quickly things could turn from good to bad. Though I didn't need to do any running, the right footwear is crucial for such environments. I would normally just go in an old pair of trainers, but someone at work convinced me it would be worth spending a bit of money on some good hiking gear, especially if I ended up clambering over rocks. I can now confirm that he was right. The expensive Merrell hiking trainers I bought before leaving have been an absolute godsend. My feet are in great condition considering what they have been through, and after acknowledging what a difference they made to previous experiences in knackered out trainers, never again will I go cheap on footwear.

March has been the perfect time of year to come to southern Morocco. I imagine the rest of the summer could be unbearably hot here and the choice of accommodation more limited when it's busy. I have seen many RVs, but only two or three tourists on foot. To avoid other tourists is one of the best aspects of arriving out of season. The southern landscape is harsh but fascinating in its way. The entire south comprises hard desert rock. It's a little too harsh and bland for me to want to return this far south, other than to the Sahara and the dunes, which could easily entice me to visit them again.

At first, there were no obvious signs of life in the desert beyond Zagora, but it surprised me to discover it was there, just hidden. I soon found out that a variety of plants, flies, and birds were thriving very well. A blackbird and its mate were my constant eloquent companions throughout the daylight hours, even coming close by once more in the morning to investigate my camp before then flying off. It was almost as if they came to say goodbye. I have found animals in Morocco to be much more friendly and less afraid than in the UK. Camels, cats, birds, and flies all come close and liked to say hello. It seems to be the Moroccan way. Dogs don't, though. Funny that. I also haven't seen a single snake or scorpion, though I wouldn't have minded. One wildlife encounter that made me jump was when a large rabbit came belting out from the palms as I foraged for fronds for my fire. The sand was also great for spotting tracks and spores, and it was exciting to get a feel for what was around me. Though I couldn't see much of it, the tracks told me plenty more was out there. If I had the time or energy, I would have surrounded my camp with smoothed sand last night to see what came by.

Other than the incident with the howling dog - which was so odd how it disappeared once I got out of the hammock - I also heard two strange noises at various points in the night, though I am not sure exactly when they occurred. The first one was a guttural and wet sounding *"glag, glag, glag"*, and it moved rapidly from one side of me to the other. It was much too fast moving to be a frog but could have been some kind of small feline, though it was an odd sound for a cat to make and the speed of movement didn't fit either. I sensed it directed the sound at me because of how it delivered it. I could almost feel it hitting me. It happened once but didn't happen again, or not that I noticed.

But the scariest moment of the night happened a long time after the barking dog incident. I came awake suddenly with the certainty that I had just heard a deep and throaty *"huff"*. I lay as still as I could, listening. Shivering from the cold, it was about 4 am, and that malevolent breeze was nipping at me with its icy teeth. Then the sound happened again. It was large, and it was close, maybe only ten feet away from my head. My immediate response was to grab for my blade and tense up my buttocks. I lay there helplessly, imagining an imminent clawing and preparing for large teeth to sink themselves into the flesh of my ass. But nothing came, and the huffing sound did not happen again. It was odd to lie there, strapped into the hammock, unable to move should something come near. The whole time stuck there with the image of a large, hungry feline predator roaming around. I felt like a prepped dinner, served neatly wrapped and unable to defend myself. My butt was hanging down, inviting anything that had fangs to take a chomp. There wasn't much I could have done. It was a curious experience to go through. I knew it was well aware of me, and I assessed within seconds all my options and knew that I had none. It was peculiar because my mind had to accept that there really was nothing I could do. A predatory animal mauling me in a hammock would not be a pleasant experience, but there wasn't a lot I could have done if it had tried.

After a while, I got used to the terror I was feeling and the expectation of it. The fear could only go on for so long, and I eventually stopped being bothered by it. I ran out of the energy needed to keep worrying. The next thing I knew, I had fallen back to sleep, or to shiver, would be a better way of putting it. But that noise had sounded powerful and deep. It sounded exactly how I would imagine the guttural emission of a big cat would sound. Maybe it figured me to be too strange, or too large, to risk biting. When I first heard it, I wanted to appear threatening or seem like too much of a challenge to bite, so had moved about violently and made my presence felt. I was also trying to locate the knife that had slipped down beside me as I'd slept. My only other line of defence - if I had to engage it - was a shrill whistle that I kept hung around my neck and had put on before I left Zagora that morning. The idea being to use it to call for attention should I fall into a ravine, or break an ankle, or become incapacitated. I had not expected to need it for scaring a big desert beast, but it might have helped. I held it in my mouth ready, while I waited with my unsheathed blade in one hand and the other clutched around my ass cheeks, preparing to wrestle whatever came at me.

Something else I have gleaned from this trip is a trick I learnt and wrote about on my trip to Spain. I seem to find exactly what I need around the next corner once I let go and flow with events as they unfold. It is noticeable because it worked so well for me this time, and this trip has been an excellent test of that theory. It may be just the luck of the traveller, or maybe something about Morocco itself. Maybe I have hooked onto the ability to float freely, and in doing so become more available to opportunity when it comes by. I can grab it with more ease than I used to, now that I've figured out the approach. And it may seem trite or unimportant, but it's something I battled with in Spain initially, yet here I seem to have perfected the art. It requires letting go of the mindset we live by back home. Letting go of all scheduling and expectations. Setting a plan for the day, but then allowing the world to change it on a whim. To adapt. Letting the flow redirect me as I travel on through, requires a trust. Not sticking with rigid planning, but putting a faith in the flow to work out. This is something I have heard gypsies use. A method of finding things when they wander cities. I think it was called *"tatting"*, but I am not sure who I heard that from. The method involves wandering, and when they get to the end of one road, they wait until they get a sign or a feeling and then take the turn, left or right, based on that.

My hotel is empty, comfy, and cheap, and I couldn't wish for better. It has everything I need or could want at this point. *Perfect*, is the correct word. Everything about this trip so far has been uncannily perfect in its way. I don't wish to jinx it, merely to take a note of it, and I shall now duly ignore that I ever mentioned it and just get on with the flow.

God bless this beautiful country and the people and spirit that exists here. I have gone from being afraid of it to respecting and loving it. There is, at its heart, a kindness here, and a kindness that you don't find in England in quite the same way. That is a big shame. People will be suspicious and shun you in England far more so than they do in Morocco, or maybe it's just because I live there and take it for granted. Out here, they want to know everything about you, and they welcome you in. This was not what I was expecting. Morocco has been an oasis in the desert of life for me, and I appreciate it for being so.

I have good friends back in London, some are in Harrow where I live and work, but I'm also alone in that. Something is changing in my life, but I'm not sure exactly what. Life has changed gear. I've aged, matured, and grow tired of the ways I've been living for two decades or more. It feels like I'm hanging around in a place that I probably should have left a long time ago, but I've forgotten how to move on when the time cam that I should.

I don't want to think about it too much while I'm here, but I have a feeling it will change again soon. My life is very different now compared to how it was when I took that last trip to Spain. It changed something in me, and it has been unfolding in my life ever since, and not always in comfortable ways. This feels like the next turning point in that unravelling. Where last time I was in a relationship, a career, owned a house, and so on, today I own very little, live in a small rented room, I'm single, and have no interest in furthering my career any more, I want out. But I haven't figured out what to do yet. It feels like I have been preparing for something these last few years. I've been adjusting, reducing things, learning indigenous ways, all while I wait to find out what my life should do next. I'm still in the same job, and maybe that is a part of the problem and why I feel stuck; I am still in the machine. But I am trying to get ready to go with the flow and to roll with it when the time comes to escape, I just haven't felt ready or seen the right signs yet. This trip has confirmed for me, that it is time to make that kind of change. I do now think that time is coming.

As the sun finally burst over the mountain this morning at dawn, and those rays of light arrived to save my sorry, shivering ass, a giant star hung in the sky above the dark mountain peaks. It was huge, bright white, and it remained visible for a long time until the growing light of a new day eventually overwhelmed it. I stood there coming back to life, and I remembered that I'd dreamed that I was told the star's name and purpose, but in my shivering state, that name escaped me. I think the star was Sirius, and from what I could recall of the dream, I had the feeling it was there to guide to me. Sometimes we need the stars to guide us, and there are many ways in which that truth can manifest into our lives.

Une Bierre

I am still sitting beside the pool at the Hotel Palmerie and have just learnt that it was the first hotel built in Zagora in the 1950s. It's an excellent choice and I like it here. Still feeling dazed and recovering from the ordeal of yesterday, but a dip in the ice-cold pool purged me of any residual numbness. I finally found some staff and have ordered a meal, and what I relish to glide me into an afternoon nap - *une bierre!* I slurp it now, so expect nonsense from me for a while.

It's a special moment to be coming in from the desert, knowing you are alive and have survived an extreme experience. The amber nectar hits me between the eyes and straight away begins to pleasantly dull my edges. I am reminded of that classic black and white movie, I think it's called *"Ice Cold in Alex"*, and is set during World War II. The scene is of three men and a woman who have been lost in the Sahara, they eventually find a small town at the edge of the desert and stagger into a bar. They order a beer and just stare at it. I'm feeling that same speechless delight. There is nothing quite like facing an ice cool beer on a hot day when you are parched. *Cheers!* Here's to me, and here's to you. Whoever and wherever you are reading this, *Gawd bless ya!*

From here on in, I intend to make it about relaxation and enjoy the rest of this brief holiday. I need to take another ride in Hell's own cab - The Grand Taxi - tomorrow, but I have achieved all the goals I set out to. I was pensive about this trip before I left. The week before leaving I was truly a bag of nerves, as I knew I couldn't wriggle out of it. I would never have forgiven myself if I hadn't come, and yet I knew things could go wrong for me by coming here. The leap was terrifying, much scarier than the trip to Spain because it was that bit further, wilder, and less familiar. I return to England with a prize, that of experience. So, for the rest of this trip, I am just content to be a passenger again, happy to take a back seat and let the wind blow me where it will. I know much of what has transpired won't sink in until I return home. It's been a fast, heady whirlwind of experience and it's been wild, all new, and invasive upon my being. It has smashed me, but taught me much. My usual reverie has been impossible other than to grab moments and commit them to paper for later digestion and consideration.

It's a country that works on fate and by the will of Allah, and that's something that isn't lost on this weary, happy adventurer. I have seen things here that I know will shape the course of my future. I know it because I can feel how they've hit me at the core of my being. It has given me something. My spirit feels revitalised by this trip, and that was exactly what I was looking for.

Another recollection comes back to me, and I put down my beer to write. It was a moment in the Sahara desert. I was sitting in the tent, lost for anything else to say to the men who might well be the last in a line of Tuareg desert people. I felt painfully aware that I was looking at the end of something ancient, and it made me feel sad to consider it. Then in the distance, I heard the *"thunk, thunk, thunk"* of a machine.

"Is that a water-well?" I asked.

"Non, that is a hotel being built. It is not good news for us." said the young Tuareg.

There is a war being waged that we few of us will grasp until it is too late. It's a war against the machine, to stop it from taking over our lives. I came to the desert to escape it, only to hear its empty, metallic heartbeat clunking away out there too. Unmistakable in its repetitive, lifeless, *"thunk, thunk, thunk"*. I am not sure we can hope to beat it, or even if we should bother trying. But just like with opiates, if we come to rely on what it gives us, and if we surround ourselves with its false promise, then we will become irreparably reliant and ensnared by it. Maybe it's too late for humanity. I suspect it is. It isn't something to bequeath to our children, and yet it's growing stronger in our midst each day. In a couple of generations, they won't even know it used to be another way here. This world will disappear, forgotten.

The machine is taking over nature, concreting over our world, and I come back to this theme over and over for good reason. My search has been to find an antidote to this disease. By travelling, I had hoped I might understand how to undo it, or discover something that could hold it off. But I don't think we can do anything to fix it, there seems something inevitable about it. Even the Sahara desert isn't safe from its reach any longer, and so I doubt anywhere is. Why? Because the machine springs from within us, it's in our mindset, and it's like a disease that we carry. It follows us wherever we go. Like a parasite, it infects everything we come into contact with. We carry it in our thinking processes, and it poisons everything we touch, further infecting every culture that we contact and we inflict it on our kids too. And so here it is among us, invisible yet feeding off us, thriving through us. And we keep it well fed and watered. It is a part of us, it *is* us, and yet it is not. I realise the beer has made me a little wobbly, and so I leave to have an afternoon nap.

After a short sleep, and when I awake, I find myself lying on the bed thinking about women *[EDIT: these years later, it read so badly that I had to remove the worst of it before publishing]*. No sooner have I penned the thoughts down upon the page and left the room for a little more sunshine, than I see a lone woman wandering around in the hotel and she accosts me (honestly, she did). She has that look in the eyes (which I can't go into detail because it *"read so badly"*, but you know the one). We talk briefly and she claims to be working at the hotel, but she's not dressed as I would expect and is wearing casual clothes. She has an upfront way about herself, which I also wouldn't expect from a hotel worker at their place of work, but who knows in Morocco.

Since she doesn't seem to be busy, nor in a rush to get off anywhere, I invite her to sit down for a drink with me and we chat for a while. It's nice to have some female company, though I admit to being surprised. Given everything the Tuareg had told me about women in Morocco being out of bounds, she is proving to be an anomaly.

Her English is not so great, but she has enough of a grasp of it that we are able to struggle through. And after a brief discourse, I have discovered a few more things about this country. Moroccans can't leave Morocco as they have no visa or passport, and it is difficult to get one. I immediately realize that a dumb and horny European might appear like a visa opportunity, and make a mental note to be cautious. I wonder if this goes some way to explain the sultry looks that I am sure I've been getting since arriving here from some of the local women. Sabrina - for that is her name - then playfully tries to persuade me I want to get drunk with her. *Hmm.*

It's a fantastic view from the terrace of Hotel Palmeria as the sun begins to drop in the afternoon sky. It's just me and Sabrina by the pool and not another soul has appeared in the hotel in the time we have been here. In the distance, dust rises from a 4x4 as it tears across the rocky landscape. As the afternoon wanes, the sandy terrain beyond the hotel walls becomes host to hundreds of turbaned men, some meandering about, some sitting to enjoy the fading sun. I contemplate marrying Sabrina just for the hell of it, maybe just to feel the experience of setting someone free. What else am I saving myself for? I just don't know. But I don't mention the idea.

I am feeling tired now, and it's hard to stay awake. It's only been half a day, but I am already finding sitting around in an empty hotel to be tedious, Sabrina's company excluded. I understand there is nothing I need to do today, and that I should relax to recover my energy for the rest of the trip, but now I have started drinking, it's made me eager to go do something or risk falling asleep.

A few beers further into our drinking session and in a moment of frothy over-excitement - and in my typically brash and obvious fashion - I invite Sabrina to my room. I don't know exactly what I am thinking, it just seems to fall out of my mouth. I'm not drunk, but I am always randy as a goat, and she has been hanging around that bit beyond what seems appropriate for just chatting. When alcohol becomes involved in my life, I become laddish, crass, and shamelessly direct. Thank the lord I don't have access to any drugs, or I might have just pounced on her. It would be just like me to get myself chased out of the country, or shot in the balls for molesting a local. But I am intrigued by that smouldering energy that lurks behind the eyes of the Moroccan women. If it isn't sexual - and if I am mistaking it - then I don't understand what it is, but I want to. The effect on me is powerful, and for all my crass misogyny, the radar rarely lies. But who knows for sure, maybe I'm just a typical male and someone should throw some cold water on me. I just want to know whether behind that sultry, smouldering eye contact thing that she has spent the last hour doing, there is a wild animal eager to get out. So, I asked...

Religious repression is famous for having explosive repercussions. I learnt that from Catholic school girls a long time ago. Morocco seems pretty religious and is strict about it, too. You can feel the Muslim vibe here. But I also know that Nature has the only set of laws that truly define human behaviour. Morality doesn't mean a damn thing, it's just a pressure cooker for Nature. And though I obey Nature's whims a little too much, she seems to know how to hold things in balance, while human morality is basically bullshit. It always was, and always will be. I know this. People make stuff up as they go along to cover their tracks and hide their carnal urges. Morality moves the goal-posts all the time, and we make excuses for our behaviour when it breaks out, but Nature never demands that of us. Nature doesn't care what we do. Nature never needs us to apologise. Nature always plays it straight down the line. That is what I love about her. We are animals lurking beneath a false veneer. Other living beings either want to feed on you, flee from you, or sometimes fuck you, and animals will just get on with trying to do one, or all, of those things. You can see it in the eyes. But we humans are fakes. We hide our genuine desires out of shame. Just watch any television show about the natural world and you can see this truth in action. Nature rules us, and she does so through our hungers. Shame is the real problem standing in the way of honesty. We are not as civilised as we try to pretend.

Sabrina and I, we are no different - there are savage animals lurking beneath the surface. I'm pretty sure I picked up on that, and pretty sure she knew it too, which is why she was waiting around long after the conversation died. Someone will always tut at me at for mentioning it; but what exactly is the issue with feeling hornier than a five-legged coyote? Why on earth do we all pretend we don't get these urges? Men and women, both. I don't get why we aren't more honest about that.

As long as I am honest about it, and don't poke it in her leg without an invitation, surely inviting her to my hotel room was okay? We had run out of things to say, and I was just throwing in fillers to keep her entertained, and she was still sitting there like she was waiting for something. But it's never a straightforward thing to figure out. No one knows what a woman is thinking. The moment you reveal your intentions and ask the question, she can switch and act outraged while knowing full well she led you up to the moment, and sometimes that is the game they then love to play. So, it's always a risk to take the lead, but men have to. That is our job. And it *is* a game, and one we are both playing.

I have only one intention, if I am honest, and that's getting my leg over. While she is probably more focused on the visa aspect of the deal. It is always a deal, because we are all merchants looking to get something. I figure a grown woman can decide for herself. Human morals and decency? Fuck human morals and decency, Nature rules the day. Morals and decency are a dishonest farce, an excuse to continue with the lies. Better to be honest. That's my theory, anyway...

The result of my invite was that she disappeared quickly after I suggested it, so maybe I got the signals all wrong, and I might have to revisit my methods on a sober head. Maybe she has gone to get the manager, or her ten protective cousins, but I'll stay and finish my drink. It was nice to have some female company for a while. Strange how she had showed up right after I had been thinking about that sultry look in the eyes of the women, and just after I had written my thesis on it *[though I wont subject the reader to the full length version, I am sure you get the picture]*.

Some random thoughts come to me as I enjoy the sunset - alone, again - and I find a staff member and order up some more beer. What will I do if Sabrina comes back with the police or a gaggle of sword brandishing cousins? Or maybe she will appear dressed in something racy with that smouldering look intensified and ready to do battle for a visa. You just never can tell. Women can go either way in the flick of an eyelash. They can turn on you in a rage of apparent disgust at the suggestion, or they can drop their clothes to the floor, only to demand why it took you so long to get around to asking. Bloody confusing creatures, which is why I felt so bad for those Tuareg lads. You need a lot of practice to deal with them. I haven't got a clue how women decide on such things, it defies all linear thought or logic, but there is only one way to find out, though it often takes work to translate the results. *Female Hieroglyphs*.

I am thinking about her exit now. She didn't say a word, just looked at me without a change of expression, then got up and left. It was hard to tell from the way she did it, if it was a yes, or a no, or a *"now you must die for your insolence, infidel pig."*

Either way, I'm not leaving here until I have finished drinking, at some point the answer will reveal itself, I am sure. I have no plans other than to keep sipping at this beer, then in a few minutes I plan to fall into that pool again, and after that I will go nestle into the soft, bouncy mattress in my hotel room, and at some point - probably after sunset - I will fall into a good night's sleep.

Some more thoughts come to me as I enjoy the descent into evening. If you could invent some portable device that uses solar power to extract water from the air, you would be onto something. Desert trips could be made more safely. Though with not a drop of dew in the mornings, it might be tough to get enough water out of the air to survive on. Maybe it's something to hit my engineering-minded father with on my return.

My one regret so far, is that I didn't tip my Tuareg desert guide, and I still feel bad about that. Before leaving the Sahara in the morning, I noticed they had a spinning weather vane on their tent, and when I commented on it, they told me that a visiting Frenchman had put it there. I tried to tell the young Tuareg about how it could power his tent, but I could see that he didn't understand what I was talking about, even though he nodded as if he had. The Sahara is crying out for the harnessing of its natural power, or so I felt in that moment. With a mixture of intense sunshine followed by vicious sandstorm winds, there's the opportunity, not to make money, but to take advantage of its climate and rugged, inhospitable terrain to escape the civilised world. Sure, the hotels will build oases for rich golfers to play with their balls in the Sahara, but they will only take up a small patch of turf and always arrive and leave by the same route; air-conditioned RVs or limousines from an airport some place. The rest of the desert will remain uninhabitable, and that makes it attractive in this over-populated world.

Another odd thing of note was the Grand Taxis regularly stopping to let people out in the middle of nowhere with not a town for miles around. I dared to ask one guy where he was going as he collected his things, and he told me his home was only a one and a half-hour walk across the desert. Only one and a half. All that way in the heat of the midday sun that had nearly killed me in just thirty minutes while carrying my rucksack. The flats he was pointing towards did not have any palm trees for shade, nothing but miles of flat rock as far as I could see. No town, no village, no huts, nor any obvious sign of a home at all, and no road leading there either. Hardy bastards, these Moroccans.

I just realised that I haven't seen a cloud since I arrived here, not even a wisp, though an ever-present dusty haze goes some way to protecting the skin from harmful UV. Until today, I haven't bothered with suntan lotion despite the thirty-five-degree blaze that I have been subjecting myself to. I thought my sunburn would be a hell of a lot worse after yesterday, but other than knocking me out because of the heat, sunburn has been no trouble at all.

I liked Sabrina, it's a shame she disappeared. There was something magic about her timely appearance, just as I was thinking about all things female. She was young, lively, and pretty, sort of, nothing that a bit of dental repair couldn't put right. I am not sure if she is missing some teeth or if they are just badly cracked. It isn't as bad as it sounds, but it's an odd look for a woman. Could happen to anyone, but in my country they would fix it immediately. It made me realise that I'm not used to seeing women with teeth issues, and I found it curiously endearing, since it's so rare to see crooked teeth in women with relative good looks. Moroccans have far too much sugar with their tea and they will pay the price. I guess her to be in her mid-twenties, but didn't ask. While her first question had been to ask if I was married. *Yikes!* But it was something the Tuareg men told me women here measure everyone by, and so was to be expected. I miss her feminine company already. Sometimes just being around one is enough when you feel starved of a good connection, and I feel starved currently, though I bet you never guessed. Especially true of times like these, while travelling alone through the wilds of a foreign world. It would have been nice to have had a drinking companion for the evening, but she still hasn't returned, so it's looking like I scared her off.

Maybe I could organise a music show in the Sahara desert. Yes, why not. Carry the gear out there by camel, no problem. I jammed with the Tuareg boys using their instruments that night. I wasn't much cop on their three-stringed guitar, but we all had a good bash of the Moroccan drums. Suddenly I want to go back to the Sahara, hang out with the lads there again. They were cool guys, down to earth. They told me about the contraband camel that does runs from Algeria that they meet to get cheap smokes and reefer. I knew that they'd love my world, and I wondered if I could bring it out to meet them. A gig in the desert. Hell, make a band video out here, maybe. I like the idea. I should at least go back and get a phone number off the guys I bought the camel trek from.

Finish up this next beer that just arrived and I might. They could help me arrange it all. Trek a party from M'Hamid to Zagora by camel, camp desert-style as we go, rocking out each night. Come to think of it, I haven't heard US or English music out here except for once at the *Camping Les Jardins* when Blondie came on the radio. I wonder what they would make of our music? Ideas come fast with this additional beer. Then I fart loudly, and it makes me laugh as it echoes off the walls. I'd forgotten that other people are now here. Only a French couple that showed up about ten minutes ago and didn't engage me, but I forgot I was no longer alone. The ripper stunned them into silence as it echoed a wonderful decay off the walls in a rhythmical fade. I smile and raise my glass. It's okay, I'm a musician. It's all about the rhythm and melody. And you're welcome.

Arabian Nights

I had an excellent dinner in the hotel and then set about demolishing a few more beers. Stork, local stuff that wasn't too bad. Some time later, I went to visit my camel trek guides. They could tell something was up from my alcohol-induced friendliness. But I got their number, which was the reason for going. Some Spaniards were in the shop when I arrived, and Hairy camel-toe's brother tried to use me to support his selling tactics. It didn't work out the way he wanted and he was soon ushering me out of the door instead. I never was much of a salesman, and he'd read me wrong again.

I returned to the hotel and was wondering whether to continue sobering up, or to get back to some more drinking, when Sabrina re-appeared. Her hair was now down, and she'd dressed herself up a bit. This answered the question that had been on my mind since she'd disappeared earlier in the afternoon. So, now I knew I'd read it right. In the low light, she looked pretty good. It certainly helped that her teeth were a lot less visible. She loitered, and I offered to get her a drink. She refused politely, but then sat down opposite me anyway. I could tell she was more concerned about being seen than she had been before, and I wondered if maybe the boss was back in. It was nice to have her company again, and I told her so. I asked her what she liked to drink, when she drank, and she said vino. Wine sounded like a good idea, so I ordered a bottle of local red and poured myself a glass. A short time later, she announced she would come to my room, but that she had to do something first. I asked her what it was but couldn't understand her reply, and I think she meant it to be that way.

I was feeling tired, but I figured a short time chatting in my room might be easier than in the hotel bar. I could also lie down to listen to her, as it had been a long day. There were more staff milling around in the hotel now the night was coming on. She could also then stop looking around shiftily to avoid whoever she was trying to avoid. Of course, I am not kidding anyone, and the possibility of getting laid would always be on my mind, but that wasn't something I ever hid. Whether we were in the bar or in my hotel room, I'd be much the same. But I genuinely hoped that I might learn more about life in Morocco from her, the women especially were such a detached and enticing mystery to me that I was eager to hear more.

Sabrina disappeared to do whatever it was she had to do, and I settled up my hotel bill. It was 80 dirham for the bottle of wine, so I bought a second bottle, and then paid a further 140 dirham for the food and beer that I'd consumed throughout the day. I then took myself and my two bottles up to my room and promptly fell asleep.

A light knocking awoke me at 10:30 pm. It was Sabrina, and I let her in. It took me a moment or two to get situated and figure out where I was, but I soon set about pouring us both some wine. There were two single beds in the room. The one I had selected to sleep in was by the window and she sat down on the bed opposite. I made myself comfortable, lying back against the pillow propped up at the head of my bed, and sipped at my drink.

Despite achieving a fair bit of conversation downstairs, now that we were in quieter surrounds and able to converse without interruption, our talking didn't seem to go anywhere. Whenever I thought she had understood something, I soon found out she hadn't. It was a bit confusing, and I wondered if I had been talking to myself the entire time. I learned little else about Morocco, but what I did discover was that she could drink like a fish. When she moved onto my bed uninvited and grabbed my hand to massage it, maybe I should have known something was up, but it felt good and so I let her. Ten minutes later, she'd finished more than half a bottle of red, a banana, and was now busy making a demand for chocolate that I didn't have. From what little I had understood from our conversation, she had a brother who was ill, and her father and mother were both dead, though she didn't seem upset to mention it, so I just nodded sagely. She also said she was 26. Anything else I tried to find out about her seemed to be met with a disinterested shrug. Not that she was being cagey, she just seemed uninterested in talking about anything, and my questions landed with not much response in return. We were down to candlelight by this time. I'd had some in my pack, which I'd lit at her request after she had asked me about what I was doing in Morocco and what was in my bag.

In my tired state, and with the dance of the flickering candlelight, she looked every bit the Arabian princess. And I watched her rubbing at my hands, feeling both enchanted and quite mesmerised by events. I'd found female company with no effort at all. A real, live Moroccan woman, was in my hotel room. If only the Tuareg lads could have seen me. Given what they had told me about Moroccan women, the opportunity to hang out with one was the luck of kings. I guess I had white privilege after all. I was lying there thoroughly enjoying the experience, happily amazed by my continued good fortune. Arabian nights. Mysterious, wild, and intoxicating. In the subdued lighting, she was a tanned, and beautiful Persian wonder, and it all felt delightfully exotic. I imagined having these experiences in the desert, a king being served by a harem of hand-massaging concubines in the dancing candlelight of Saharan bedouin tent. I couldn't have asked for a more pleasant way to end to the adventures of the last few days.

I smiled up at her, trying not to fall asleep. Why was life not like this more often? Then, suddenly, she made a grab for my groin and lunged her face in towards mine to kiss me. It was all so unexpected that it took me off guard and it felt strangely rushed and stumbled. It was odd for a woman to be taking the lead, and it felt jarring somehow. But I was so intoxicated by the mood, the wine, and the heady wonder of it all, that I had no reason *not* to go along with it, so I did. I'd barely gotten a hand to a breast before she was struggling with my clothes in return. Even by my standards, it was rapid, but she set the pace and I saw no reason to complain about that. It was past midnight, and my hangover was threatening through the wine haze, and then there was the infuriating niggle of knowing that I needed to be up at 6 am to make Ouarzazate in good time. Unsurprisingly, the next stage didn't take long, and no sooner had it all begun than it was over.

"You give me now five hundred dirham," she said,

climbing naked off the bed.

"Eh?" I replied.

It was so abrupt and jarring, that I thought she was joking and made light of it. She repeated herself, and it turned out she was not joking. I went through a range of emotions in the space of a millisecond. A Moroccan haggle then ensued, while my mind went over what kind of shit I might be in if I refused to give her a single cent, which was my intention in that moment. I was feeling quite put out.

"It's for the hotel," she said.

"What? Did the hotel put you up to this?" I asked.

"Oui," she replied.

For a moment I thought I was in deep shit. Were men with swords outside my door waiting for her signal? My mind reeled, trying to understand everything that I had missed about Sabrina. She had given me no hint of this being a money deal, and I told her so.

It was then that I noticed something in her method. I paused and held her in a long gaze, trying to assess the creature. Had I just glimpsed an amused look lurking behind the serious expression? Yes, there it was again. Sabrina was playing with me. She was trying to see what she could get. When I considered it further, I thought it more likely that *she* would be in trouble, and not me, if the incident came out. I relaxed then, but needed to be certain.

I told her to wait where she was, then I put on my boxer shorts, got off the bed, and went to the door and opened it. Peering out, I checked up and down the corridor, but no one was there. How could I have been so stupid not to see through her machinations? Her overt openness, her willingness to come to my room, the gifted massage, the disinterest in making conversation, then her grabbing at my bits. I had been dumb. *Arabian princess?* yea, right? Gappy toothed prozzie was more like it.

She wanted me to call her from England and gave me her phone number and an email address, but I was agreeing to everything just to get her to leave. I felt duped, though I wasn't sure why it mattered. I'd got what I wanted. So we began haggling, and I got her down to 100 dirham, and I was surprised when she seemed content to leave it at that. I told her she had drunk the wine, eaten my bananas, smoked my cigarettes, and that it all added up. She didn't ask for anything else after that, and I got the feeling she hadn't been expecting any money at all.

On the way out, she persuaded me to part with another packet of cigarettes, and then she stole a kiss at the door. I was going along with it to get her out of my room, hoping it was nearly over and that I could finally go to bed. Standing, blocking the doorway so she could not get back in, I watched her go down the corridor, and even gave her a wave when she turned at the end. I then waited a few moments, just to be sure she was gone. I then went back inside, closed the door, locked it, and put a chair underneath the handle. Then I went to the bathroom. I could picture the Tuareg boys laughing.

By All The Gods

I got up and paid my room bill and escaped without further incident. I now sit waiting, what could be hours, for a Grand Taxi to fill and take me the four-hour journey back to Ouarzazate. If I make it there on time, then on to Marrakech, and from there a train to Casablanca tomorrow. If I am delayed, then I will have to take the plane from Ouarzazate back to Casablanca in a day or two. It's best to have back-up plans ready just in case, but I have enough wiggle room to still go with the flow.

I recall last night. What an idiot. Intoxicated, not just by the booze but by romantic delusions. Pleasure in life always comes at a price, and it's often short-lived. Lofty ideals followed by a grand fall back down to earthly realities. But life is full of paradox, and I think it important to separate the two aspects of any experience, and not allow one aspect to poison the memory, or let it sink us in shame. It's all about the adventure, and what an adventure it has been. Some of the worst decisions of my life have become my favourite memories. Time heals pretty much everything, and often the rough stuff ends up making us laugh the longest. Later, though, a lot later. I need to re-frame the events of last night. They left me feeling tricked and duped, but really I shouldn't feel that way about it, and I don't want to. Once again, on demand, Morocco delivered to my door exactly what I had asked for. I consider that now.

After Sabrina left, I soon fell asleep. I then dreamt of a woman I wanted to be with years ago. In the dream I saw her at a bus garage in Bampton, the village near to where we both grew up. She was driving a Mini and had her daughter with her, who looked to be about eight years old. The woman didn't see me at first. So I went over, but once she recognised me, she gave me a look of what I took to be disdain. I tried to say hello, but she was non-committal and unresponsive. The rebuff hurt me deeply.

The last time I saw her in real life was a long time ago, and she'd been cold to me then too. I think in some dark corner of my mind she became the one that got away. Sometimes she'd show up in my dreams, and she'd be dismissive when she did. I'm sure that meant something, though I'd never deciphered what. But on this occasion, it wasn't the end of the dream.

After acting dismissively toward me, I assume her feelings are the same as ever, and I make to leave.

"Don't be silly," she says. "Nothing ever happens around here. It's boring. Please. Stay."

A surge of happiness washes over me. After all these years lost in a solitary wilderness, I have finally been allowed in. She feels like home and where I belong. I watch her blue eyes, surprised at the change of heart, but it's genuine and it overwhelms me to know this. She smiles at me, finishes filling her car with petrol, and then walks to the cashier to pay. She's exactly the same as I remember her - slender, tall, elegant, and beautiful. Her daughter sits waiting in her car, distracted by something in her lap, maybe a game. A wonderful feeling is on me, and I wake.

The sensation remains with me now as I wait in the dust of the busy taxi rank at Zagora, and I smile to myself. It's a good day today.

The Grand Taxi eventually leaves at 9.30 am and we arrive in Ouarzazate around 12:30 pm. I'm been put in the boot with a Frenchman. It's piloted by an amateur formula-one driver, and the car is the worst I have taken so far. The floor of the taxi is rusty and broken and the exhaust pipe is leaking in. This causes the toxic air to accumulate in the back more than anywhere else. At one point, while climbing the winding slopes beyond Agdz, a sharp left-hander taken too fast fills the car up with smoke. It has been killing us slowly anyway, but now we can't even see out of the windows, but this doesn't slow our driver down. Finally, someone gets a window down for a short time before others insist it gets rolled back up. When I ask if they can leave it down, they all refuse, and I am told by the Frenchman that the Moroccans believe the wind is evil. The rest of the trip is an awful experience, and it adds more *mal-a-tete* to my already savage hangover.

I am in a foul mood and feeling disorientated, it's the first time I have been in this bad a rage since arriving in Morocco. My head is pounding from the intoxication, and it's ruined the stunning views of the journey. There had been some interesting sights, like the flat top of a mountain we passed shaped like a heart, and my first sighting of a cemetery - a simple affair, recognisable by the body-sized mounds with small pyramid stones placed on each, all pointing skyward. No mausoleums, cherubs, or marble tombstones here, but something more affordable and desert suitable. Then, as we reach the outskirts of Ouarzazate, I see a plastic bag mountain and plastic bag trees, all of it blown there by the wind and accumulated over the years. It looks like the birth place of plastic bags and they grow on trees.

I spot the CTM bus garage and cry out for the driver to stop.

"ICI, S'IL VOUS PLAIT MONSIEUR!"

At long last, I can escape the mobile death trap.

Heading first to the café beside CTM, there I try to recover my composure and go to take a leak. Things don't improve as I enter the worst smelling dirty, dank, and unlit toilet that I have ever had the displeasure to be in. It's a record-setter, and I find myself instantly transported to the bowels of Hell.

After drinking a litre of water on the journey just trying to stay alive, I've been busting for a pee for three hours, and so it takes an age to get it out of me. I stand pissing into the blackness and what I hope is the hole. Creepy spiders hang in shards of light from a small broken hole somewhere above my head. A palpable stench gags in the back of my throat like rotting fur, and I wonder if faecal particulate is attaching itself to my tonsils. I have slipped into a horror-show, and all the while my head pounds so hard I can hear it thumping.

As I stand there listening to the blood pulse through my head, and my pee splatting somewhere down below, I contemplate the eternity of purgatory and how on earth I came to be there. Have I offended the gods this morning? Since getting in that cab, everything has been markedly grim and unpleasant, and yet the day started out with so much promise. I consider for a moment what potential *faux pas* I might have made, and just one springs to mind that might be working against me - I didn't say goodbye to Zagora, nor did I thank the place for my time there. Is my insolence being punished?

I had spent the morning waiting in Zagora thinking about lost loves, my current sexual dilemmas, and my thumping hangover. In thinking only of myself, I had completely forgotten to follow the protocol that I had set at the beginning of this journey. I had forgotten an elemental truth about my situation. That I travel with no support other than the spirit of a place, its gods, maybe its demons, but always at its mercy. I flow in the vein of its heart-beat, and I need to appreciate that. Not much else protects me out here. I could disappear, and no one would know I was gone. *This. Is. Africa.* One should never forget that. It's a land alive with spirits, and humming with unique and diverse energies, but it can also be extremely cruel when it wants to be.

My never-ending pee is still falling into the void, and I brace against the horror of the time it's taking to finish. I have plenty of it with which to consider my situation and mistakes in life. It's the most magnificent setting for doing so.

Was the guy I saw getting knocked down on the bicycle as we left Zagora a reminder to be respectful as I made the return journey? Right now, trapped as I am in this blacked-out shitter, I feel it might have been. I decide that I must make amends for my carelessness. Christ almighty! How much longer must I stand here doing this?

My bladder finally allows me to escape the bog of eternal stench, but I am not in a good way, and I sit in a nearby café trying to suck oxygen back into my brain. I look around, wary of being accosted by Moroccans, but I am blending in well enough here, and no one appears to be staring at me or preparing to sell me anything. Since I'm not being observed, I touch my hand to my heart and then to my head in respect, and quietly begin offering my apologies to Zagora for my rudeness at leaving without saying thank you or goodbye. I don't know if my gesture is enough, but I shut my eyes and focus a little more on my feelings, try to gauge if there's more that I should do. Nothing else springs to mind, and so now it's time to say hello to Ouarzazate.

I stay in the café for a long time with my headache not improving. I try to think about what I need to do in practical terms. In a little over nine hours, the next bus to Marrakech will leave. It's a long journey, but one I won't survive if I get a Grand Taxi like the last one. The bus seems a preferable option, but will it be full of strange men and their goats? I do not know, but it's a plan.

Now, I need to address this headache that won't budge. I also need to do all I can to make the return journey free from divine intervention, shocking bogs, major errors of judgement, prostitutes, and carbon monoxide poisoning. It's also time to think in spiritual terms.

While I wait to recover, I rub my feet, hoping a little reflexology might shift the relentless thump going on in my brain. I will be dysfunctional until it lifts. I find a painful spot on my right heel. It feels like bruising and I rub at it. The exquisite pain overbears my headache and it's a relief to have the pain at the opposite end of my body for a moment. I continue hurting my feet, noticing that I can think while I do it, but not when I stop.

It's 3 pm, and I am coming around finally. The last few hours I spent wandering around and then sat by a mosque for a while. I figured it to be sacred land and respect could be made there, which felt like the right thing to do. For now, I continue to sit around and meditate on where I am at. I am definitely feeling better. There had been a nagging sensation that I needed to do something, to honour something, to give gratitude for something, and I wasn't even sure what it was. But after a while spent near the mosque considering such things, something in me shifted, and now I feel a lot less anxious. I'm feeling more like I have arrived, and I'm wondering what to do for the rest of the day.

Ouarzazate - as I discover from a quick wander - is an ex-Foreign Legion outpost and still has a marked military presence, though they seem to be Moroccan, not French. Maybe the military presence has something to do with why I haven't been accosted here as much as I was in Zagora.

The town of Ouarzazate seems much more affluent than I assumed when I arrived at the start of my trip, and its shops closer to what I am used to seeing back home. More and more, I notice European women here, either solo, or in twos and threes. A few are with dull-looking white male partners, and in observing them, I suspect it's the women who wear the trousers in most cases. What attracts so many women here? There is a definite type, but I wouldn't know how to describe them adequately. But I think I know why they come here. On the hell-ride from Zagora, a Henna-tattooed, Henna hair-died, cheap trinket wearing French woman was in the car with her French husband, he was the one next to me in the boot. They had a young black Moroccan boy with them, whom it gradually dawned on me was the woman's toy-boy. It was odd to witness, and the Frenchman was clearly quite the obedient cuckold from the way she treated him. I am thinking Morocco is for women, what Thailand is for men, and good luck to them for it, if that's their bag.

The Kefta Tagine that I just ate has given me lethal wind. I hope I have space and it is comfortable enough to sleep on the bus tonight. I won't arrive in Marrakech until 1 or 2 am, and I may have to head straight to the train station as my only option for rest at that time of night.

I can't seem to think of anything to do in this town that would interest me to pass the time. Shopping and sightseeing aren't my thing, and this leaves me no option but to sit it out and enjoy the long wait in the hot afternoon sun. I check my watch. It says it's thirty degrees. I then decide to go and find an Internet café and let friends know I'm still alive. I'm a little surprised myself. All the irrational fear I was showing the week before leaving on this adventure left me thinking I was heading to my doom. It seems silly now, because it has all been so much fun. Now that I am feeling more familiar with Morocco, it seems a lot less terrifying, and I wonder what the fuss was all about. The unknown does funny things to the mind.

I'm experiencing a strange discomfort at being back in the towns. There is no nature here, and I miss it. I can see the desert beyond, and it's even more sparse and flat out there than it was around Zagora. It's not so inviting, and I wouldn't go camping here.

This town seems to offer nothing but overbearing heat when I wander around for too long. Cars and trucks go by, and I sit on the main drag and observe people as they come and go. I am in neutral as the world turns about me. It's busier and more modern, but still a million miles away from what I am used to in London.

I am still suffering from the listlessness of my three-hour fumigation. Nothing seems to inspire me to move, so I sit outside a café and drink normal tea with no sugar. I try to listen to nature above the noise of traffic and the people talking. I can hear birds chirping in nearby trees, and so I focus on that. It's a fun respite. I notice it takes a shift in perception to maintain my attention on the sound of the birds above the street sounds.

I saw a big lizard on the journey from Zagora. It was quite a Jurassic looking beast and was lying still, basking in the sun on a rock beside the road. It looked perfectly fitting in that hot, rocky landscape. Just like a dinosaur; ancient in design and perfectly created to enjoy such harsh conditions. The desert is a reptilian land, where nothing green, soft, or human can survive long. A place where nature doesn't seem to be, but she is there, she just hides herself well. Though it is a place where life is always on the brink of disappearing. The best option for survival in the desert is to either hide beneath the sand, or make like a rock. But there *is* life in the desert, and it would surprise people to know just how much. It's not the dead place I assumed it to be. I think the desert *itself* is alive, and people need to consider that before they fill them with solar panels in the future.

I am seeing that a more cosmopolitan type of Moroccan lives in Ouarzazate. It doesn't feel so wild here. Maybe that is why it bores me. It's not soulless, it's just got nothing obvious that draws me to want to know more. I'd sooner listen to those birds chattering away in the trees. They are talking about a world different to this one, another world, that is right here and accessible to *them*. Beyond this place that man has built with his machine. *Thunk, thunk, thunk*, I can hear endless engines. *Yack, yackety, yack*, the mindless babble of people's voices. It's the drone of the living-dead. Inanimate objects go by brought to life by burning something once natural and alive. *Consumption*. Either of diesel, fuel, or food. Consumption of energy is required to remain here; the life-force must be stolen from something else living for us to survive another day. The machine eats nature, but when nature is gone, when it's used up, the machine will come to a halt, too. I contemplate this, as I listen to the birds chirping away in the trees with my eyes shut and the hot sun beaming down onto my face.

I recall again my solo adventure in Spain two years ago. It culminated in Tarifa, with me looking out across the waters at what I now know was Morocco. I recall thinking that the true heart of Arabia was in North Africa. I don't know why I thought about it at the time, it was just an odd notion I had while there. I mention this now, because I just discovered that King Mohammed VI of Morocco is a descendant of the Prophet, so they say.

As I write this down, the mosque call begins, as if in synchronised agreement with my thoughts. But cosmopolitan Ouarzazate doesn't come to a stop for the faithful like it did when I was in Jeddah many years ago, nearly getting locked in a shop during their prayers at lunchtime. Here the machine takes precedent, and it continues to hum. The machine is modernity's one true god.

I am not a great fan of Islam, but I admire some elements of its faith. They seem to hold a truer memory for what I believe is a mostly forgotten truth - that of the indigenous ways. In that regard, I admire it over Christian mumbo jumbo which, from a very young age, I knew was selling false stories. But at its heart, unfortunately, Islam seems to be just another militant religion, too. Archaic, old, not in keeping with the conditions of modernity, and it seems far better suited to another time, that of the Middle-Ages. Give me nature any day of the week. Nature is my church. She holds my holy ground and is the place I go to offer my prayers. Through her, I find a connection to my gods. In nature, I find the source of life itself, not in holy literature. Literature is empty. It's a reflection on truth. And so it's automatically second-hand thinking and therefore a false interpretation by default, nothing more. Becoming literate is considered a hex in some cultures (Malidoma's Dagara tribe, for example). It's a virus of the mind that can be learnt, but cannot be unlearned. It's the blueprint from which man has built the machine that will kill him, or consume him, or, more likely, it will merge into him and change him beyond recognition and man will become part machine. All this because of our desperate longing to achieve immortality.

Where did it all begin? In the Quran? Hardly. In the Bible? Hardly. Before them, it was mostly polytheistic religions that led us: Hinduism, Buddhism, Paganism, *etcetera*. And they had ever-expanding pantheons of gods that made them far more accepting of other people's belief systems. That is how it should be, we should be accepting of other beliefs and incorporate them into ours, maybe. While all the monotheistic religions prefer to wage war to win people over by force. Often with the sword, or at least with coercion through guilt and peer-pressure, but it's the use of force all the same. There is nothing more pious or violently insistent, than a believer in one god.

And before the oldest of religions, what was there? I can tell you - it was the animist and indigenous ways and for millions of years. Like Voudou, that deals directly with nature, spirits, and the elements. Malidoma Somé and his Dagara tribe in Burkina Faso, or Martin Prechtel and his Guatemalan tribe, all now long since murdered or run out of their homeland by the militia. Their stories went back to the beginning but not much had changed.

I don't want to deny people their faith in monotheistic organised religions, nor do I wish to misjudge some of their better aspects, but I think we should question the things we are told to take on faith through literature. It's mostly crap leftover from a coercive medieval era. There has been an adulteration of the information that they have given us to build our faiths upon. Literature is open to misinterpretation in a way that the language of nature is not. Literature is second-hand information. Nature, on the other hand, offers a more direct connection, and a personal one. Just get out there and discover it for yourself. How can there be a lie if there are no middle-men? And how can there *not* be a lie if there is? In what way should we meet with our gods? And whom should choose our gods for us? *We* should choose them, of course.

Reconnecting with nature isn't about finding a simplistic escape from reality, nor is it about trying to live off-grid, in clothes made of hessian sackcloth, awhile engaging people with fake smiles, fake intimacy, or the thousand-yard stare. I am talking about the heartbeat of nature, the paradoxical truth found through experiencing her directly. She will devour us in the end, but she is perfectly honest about that, and she does not lie.

I can understand the needs of the faithful disciples of monotheistic organised religions, and I can understand what it gives them in return. But I'm not one of them, and never will be, because to me it's based on obvious fallacy and lies. Islam, the Christian or Jewish Bible, are all just tales of morality. And morality is all about power and control of the masses, not the truth.

It is now 5:10 pm, and finally my headache and listlessness have fully lifted. Let it be noted that three hours of gassing will require five hours of recovery time. That was no fun at all. But now that I am feeling fit and back to a relative state of normality, it's time to investigate this town that I find myself in. I don't stand out in Ouarzazate, and the anonymity is welcome. I could have believed that I was the first white man to arrive in Zagora, though I certainly wasn't. Neither was I the first guy to buy a carpet there. I did that, didn't I? How funny. So, it seems they had me pegged after all. Never underestimate the Moroccans.

And now I feel it's time to move, though I don't know where yet. First, I will post the postcards I have written, and while I do that, I will have a think about what to do with myself for the next few hours in Ouarzazate before my bus leaves. I expect that if I just go with the flow, then something will to invite me to engage.

Movie Town

I posted my letters and then stopped by a shop where I'd been accosted earlier in the day when the taxi dropped me off. I'd enjoyed the banter of the lad who had stopped me, and I'd promised him I would return when I felt better. It was time to have a go at haggling again, and to get some gifts for those back home who had requested them. But my plans soon took another detour, as they tend to in Morocco if you let them.

I found the shop on Blv Mohammed V, and the young man was in there. His name was Omar. He sat me down and then produced all the usual tourist pap to sell me. It's the same everywhere, and so is the sales ritual.

"I give you final best deal price, my friend!"

bla, bla, bla.

He started at 520 dirham and I started at 100 dirham, and we met in the middle at 320 after a long journey through some hilarious bullshit.

Haggling is a lot of fun when you get into it, and in Morocco you eventually realise that you have no choice. The trick is to get animated and bullshit them right back. Tell them it's junk and that it looks like their mother's, brother's, wife's child made it, and that it's obviously not genuine. Don't be overtly rude, but be argumentative and take nothing at face value, but do it with your tongue in your cheek the entire time. The more emotional and animated you can get, the more they love it. It's a game, and they know it, and when you get into it, suddenly it all makes sense.

I ended up with a three-pronged southern cross necklace for my shrine at home, and two small camel dolls for friends, as well as spurious other insignificant items as gifts. Omar then threw in a free rock, alleging it to be a fossil. He'd probably picked it from the road just outside the shop, but I was content with my purchases. We drank tea and chatted for a little while longer, then at some point his "brother" came in.

His brother's name was Karim. He was the owner of the shop and was around thirty years old, a charismatic character. He offered me a shot of his finest Ballantine Scotch whisky, and it seemed rude not to. To impress him I necked it in one go, and I could see his eyes light up as he poured us both another. The second was an even larger shot, but I took my time with that one. I knew I'd won him over. Before long, we were chatting about everything. Karim seemed well educated and his English was excellent, probably even better than mine, and he soon persuaded me to go with him for a drink at a local bar. It was about 7:30 pm by this time, and I figured I had the time to spare for a quick one before the bus left.

It was a short walk to Bar Obelix, where we headed upstairs above the restaurant and into an archetype Arabian decor club setting. It had soft red lighting, incense smoke filled the room, and soft silk cushions surrounded the outer walls. Hookahs were available of the smoking kind. There was loud dance music, the same as could be heard in any English club. I felt immediately at home. The bar was devoid of any people when we arrived, but he knew the barman and we set about ordering drinks and talked while we propped up the bar, and gradually the place came to life around us.

Seven Ballantines later, and Karim and I were the best of friends. I'd also met half of Ouarzazate and missed my bus. In exchange for deciding to stay drinking with him, he promised me a night beyond my wildest dreams and a lift the next day from a friend who was going all the way to Casablanca, if I wanted it. I knew I could catch another bus in the early morning, but if I missed that one too, then the lift would be my back-up plan. I thanked him for it, and accepted the offer. He seemed pleased, and we ordered another drink to celebrate.

What I didn't like at first, but now love about Morocco, is that it is impossible to be alone for very long. Someone always wants to say hello, and after a few moments of conversation, invariably they invite you somewhere else. Such openness would rarely happen in England, and I was warming to the places that I was finding. I just kept having a good time without trying. People just want to open doors for you in Morocco. They want to know what you want, and what you desire, and then they will try to find it for you, or know a man who can. It's wonderful. And it's all done in such a genuine way that it makes you feel good, as if you belong there.

Karim and I bonded over our mutual love of good music, bad women, and, of course, alcohol. He must have introduced me to upwards of twenty local Moroccans in the bar that night. At some point, it filled up with various European filmcrew types too, and then I found myself dancing with a gorgeous Moroccan lady who offered to take me to Casablanca the next day at 3 pm. *How was all this happening?* I got her to write her mobile number on my arm, and she had to do it in eye-liner as neither of us could find a pen. She was stunningly attractive, and I was punching well above my weight. I'd spent hours trawling clubs in London without speaking a single soul, yet out here, everyone seemed to be so open and friendly it was making me realise what an inhospitable city I lived in.

I wandered back to the bar where Karim was still holding court, happy in his princely position, and ordering up drinks for the group as required. When I got back, he smiled knowingly at me.

"She is nice," he said, implying that he had been keeping an eye on me, and that he knew her, and he approved of the match. I guess everyone knew everyone in this town.

Someone introduced me to Karim's uncle. A man even more charismatic than Karim, if that was possible. I noticed a shadow fall over my new found friend at this point. There was definitely some rivalry going on between them. The uncle was older and just as enchanting, and I could see Karim seethe with envy when he took control of the group conversation. It got intense. And as I got more drunk, so my already paper-thin diplomatic skills went right out of the window, and I started commenting on things that I should not have.

It would not be the first time that I foolishly brought up my drunken views on religion, racism, sex, politics, family feuds, and pretty much any thought that came into my head regarding whoever, or whatever, I was observing. Even with the best of intentions, once I get drunk, it drives me towards confrontational moments and I get belligerent. There's a golden rule regarding travel, and I wish I had heard it a long time ago: *never discuss religion, sex, or politics.* I recommend sticking to this rule. The drunken revelry was fun, and most of the people I met were lovely, but as the night wore on there were some hints of racism coming at me from certain quarters, or so I felt. Whenever it happened, I was compelled to mention it. Karim had to shut me up several times, and thank god that he did. He also clarified that he didn't want to discuss Allah while drinking, even if I did. And though I saw no good reason for that, he was adamant about it.

I soon discovered that for all their openness, Moroccans can become quite touchy when you press the wrong buttons. As long as I stayed off certain topics and I didn't get too intrusive, then all was be well. This made sense to me sober, but seemed ridiculous to me when drunk. Being an obnoxious pain in the ass is something of a gift. I've had several bar fights because of it. They start over meaningless comments and then escalate, and the one thing they always involve is alcohol. My quizzing of one barman got a little heated when I accused him of giving me shifty looks. I felt he was, but it had started when he had told me he didn't have a pen, when I saw that he did. I wanted to know why he had a problem with me. It was descending to the place where trouble occurs. I was too drunk and needed to acknowledge that *I* was the problem, not other people. Karim separated us and then spent some time pacifying the upset barman.

On the whole it was a great night, but I think the dark-side needs a bit of a mention since it's often lurking about some place and looking for a way in. Booze is that way in, and though I used to enjoy the effects, I'm not sure that I do any longer, and there is a certain sense of "own what you did" required in writing this. I've had more drunken punch-ups in more random bars than I care to remember, and I suspect I would've had at least one more that night if Karim's presence had not been protecting me.

We finally left Bar Obelix at closing time with another buddy of Karim's who had just bought a new Jeep and was eager to show it off. From there they took me to a fancy hotel where they claimed 50 Cents was staying while filming his latest music video. He wasn't in the hotel, and when I discovered this, my gangster impression amused Karim as I chastised him for his mistake.

"I should pop a goddamn cap in yo' punk ass!" I said.

After that, both Karim and his pal kept doing it back to me. We had a drink by the pool, since we were there, and then left the hotel bar and stopped by Karim's house so he could change out of what he called his "tribal clothes".

It was here that I noticed Karim didn't look after himself at all well. Empty bottles of cough medicine were littered about the place, not for coughing but for drinking. It wasn't exactly a healthy living space. I realized that, even though we were having fun, maybe neither of us were the happiest of specimens, and we both sought our escape through drink, drugs, and sweet oblivion in one form or another. I guess it was the underlying reason we had bonded.

He showed me to the spare room where he said I could sleep. Thinking that was the end of the night, I put my rucksack against a wall and pulled out my sleeping bag, but when he came back in and saw me setting up for bed, he wouldn't have it. A few moments later we were off to find the next club, but I'd lost my energy by this time and was seriously cut to the wind from all the whisky. Unfortunately, "no" was not an option.

I have vague recollections of some god awful, trashy discotheque, and fending off Moroccan queers and over-friendly whores. It was a horror show compared to the Bar Obelix, and the night deteriorated rapidly. I'd had enough of the place within a short time of arriving at what was a cheesy Morrocan disco with 80's and Euro music, and so I drank more to blot it all out. I recall at some point being sprawled in a chair somewhere deep inside the place, barely able to focus and wondering how in the hell I got so fucked up.

We finally left at 4 am, once I could stand up enough to focus and hunt down Karim, who was still fully functional and was holding court with a gaggle of fans around him at the bar. He was put-out by my request to leave, but I couldn't take any more of it, and I made that clear.

I got to my sleeping bag blind drunk, confused by how my state had deteriorated so badly, though it should have been obvious. I managed not to puke, though a dark mood was on me and I was no longer fun to be around. I woke at 8 am, packed and stepped over a sleeping Karim who mumbled something about shutting the door on the way out. I think we'd both had enough of each other by then.

I don't recall how I found it, but I got to the CTM to discover the morning coach to Marrakech was about to depart. I stumbled around trying to buy a ticket and had to go back to get another one for my rucksack, before boarding to collapse in a seat somewhere near the back. The hangover was rasping violently inside my head. As we moved out, I realised I was hungry but stupidly had bought neither food nor water. I had no choice but to fall asleep and hope that the journey passed by quickly.

We headed north, north-west out of Ouarzazate towards the Atlas mountains. It was at least comfortable with the cool air-conditioning, and there was plenty of room. It made an enormous difference compared to the horrors that a Grand Taxi would have held for me in that state. And though I was hurting, I realised that, once again, things were going okay. Luck was with me still, and I'd certainly had a memorable time.

I recalled moments from the night. One in particular, was of seeing the sexiest of belly-dancers. I couldn't place where this had happened. Maybe she was dancing in the Bar Obelix restaurant when we left. Had we been in there for a while? I think we had. She'd held my attention transfixed for quite some time. It was like nothing I had seen before. She epitomised the essence of feminine beauty and moved like a snake. Recalling it brought a smile to my face, and I slumped against the window of the coach and drooled. I'd had a good time for most of the night, at least. I just wished that I didn't become such an asshole beyond that certain point, but whisky always invoked the beast.

As we left Ouarzazate, I spotted a huge studio set built out in the desert beyond the town. I could see the walls of a castle, and life-sized Egyptian pyramids. Scaffolding was holding up various other bits of scenery from behind. Beyond that, about a kilometre further out, was a gigantic fort, and then nothing, until the distant snow-capped mountains. I'd seen the same view in movies many times, and it was stunning with those snow-capped mountains as a back-drop. I could see why it had been chosen as a set location but had then turned into a more permanent fixture. It looked grand and exciting out there. It also explained why the town was more cosmopolitan and lively - Ouarzazate was a movie town.

An hour later, we began the climb into the Atlas's mountains to the north. The view then became lush with vegetation instead of the dry scorched look of the desert. As we climbed higher, I saw tumbling rivers, and it all looked so magical and refreshing. I felt like I'd been lost in the desert for years. I dozed in and out of a fitful state and was nowhere near recovery, but I didn't feel sick, so that was something. In the brief moments I opened my eyes to steal looks at the landscape, I considered how those mountains would be a great place to come to trek and camp, they offered so much more diversity than the southern deserts had. Eagles flew in the skies above, and it was stunning scenery to travel through. Even in the state that I was in, I could appreciate it.

I realized how my perspective of beauty had changed as I had gotten older. In my youth, such places had no meaning or relevance to me. I'd wanted the wildlife of the city, the craziness of the human zoo, not the boring countryside. But with maturity and a certain depth of spirit developing, it made me appreciate these sorts of place so much more now. The view that presented itself at my window, as I climbed higher into the mountain realms, was one that I longed to be in and to be a part of. It was nature.

I woke at 11:30 am when we stopped at a small mountain village for a break. Checking my watch, it told me we were at 1300 metres above sea level. It was peaceful and still, and the air was cool and fresh compared to what it had been for the last few days. So much so that it came as a shock to descend the bus steps into an atmosphere of such purity and ease. It was refreshing, and I sucked the bracing mountain goodness into my lungs. The bustle and hassle of pace in the desert lowland towns highlighted to me further the obvious choice to make these mountains my destination the next time. There was no dust. It was clean, and it felt healthy in the most natural and invigorating way. I came to life almost immediately in the cool, mentholated, oxygenated atmosphere. We were then told by the driver that we had time to eat.

I sat down outside a café that was on the main road running through the small mountain village. I noticed some children were hanging about some distance away, but they didn't pester me or vie for my attention like the kids in the desert towns had done. It was an altogether more soul-relaxing vibe in the mountains, and that made for a pleasing change of pace. An old man wandered past me and stopped to say, "Bonjour".

Somehow it felt unexpected coming from him, and I was taken aback, but said hello in return. He crossed over the quiet road and sat down on the ground on the other side, staring into space and warming himself in the sun. He was dressed like Obe-Wan Kenobi, in a dark green robe, but what struck me about him was an ornate Persian blade that he carried at his side. I fancied him to be some kind of tribal elder. He must have been two hundred years old if he was a day. His gait had been slow but gentle, and there was a defined strength to his movements. He seemed robust, and his presence held me captivated. It was the sense of calm strength that exuded from him that fascinated me the most, and the ornate blade at his side gave me the impression that his mind was equally as sharp. Having it there, added a different dimension to the man, compared to the many other Obe-Wan's I'd seen on the trip that were dressed much the same way, albeit usually in brown. He was the first I'd seen in dark green robes. Each move he made was purposeful, and he seemed efficient in a way that only the old and wise can attain. Maybe it was his age, or his wisdom, or maybe it was that ornate blade, but something shone out from him, and I couldn't stop looking. His eyes held a life and energy that matched the seclusion of the mountains and the natural world. I watched him the entire time that I ate, fascinated by him.

I have considered before that the machine has a hard time existing in the mountains because it cannot easily rid the mountains of nature. It's a lot harder to control her there than it is down in the lowlands. They always say in a time of crisis and war to *"run to the hills"* because they're a good place to hide, the mountains can protect life and nature.

It was time for us to go, and I journeyed on with the old man on my mind. He represented something important to me; he reflected the very thing I had come to Morocco and North Africa to find and maybe I had finally found it in *him*. The food had shaken me from my zombified, alcohol-poisoned state, and it brought me back to life somewhat. But in doing so, I was now having to experience the hangover at full force and was no longer numb to it. I leaned against the window and let the pain wash through me. *Why did I do this to myself? Was I really enjoying it, or was I just in denial and numbing the pain?* There was a certain addictive quality to my behaviour that was not lost on me.

As we crossed the highest point of the mountains, the colour of the land to the north lost its desert yellow-grey and became a bright pink instead. It was sudden, and the shift made it look incredible. Soon my eyes adjusted to this new hue, and then it seemed to become a more subtle brownish-pink. Then I could see pockets of yellow again, on more distant ranges, where homes were cut into the land and the colour contrast highlighted how the people lived there as a part of the earth. With each village we passed through being made of pink earth, the next one would be yellow from the earth. The adobe homes merged perfectly with their surroundings and changed right along with it. It was the definition of natural beauty to witness it.

We finally broke the High Atlas range at about 1 pm and then descended into mile after mile of flat land again. But the landscape was completely different on the north of the mountains, and it was much greener. Trees, cacti, plants, and flowers could be seen almost everywhere. Though not lush, exactly, life could grow more easily here. The earth was desert still, mostly dirt and rock, but the signs of life were more abundant.

I make Marrakech and bail out of the air-conditioned coach into a hot, dry and smelly, traffic-ridden city. Immediately deciding that I will not be hanging about in Marrakech, I then take a Petty Taxi - one that runs within the city limits - to La Gare, and from there I book the next train to Casablanca, due to leave at 3 pm. It is 2 pm when I book it, and then I go to get some more money and find somewhere to crap, hopefully in a clean café.

I check my cash and discover I am down to my last fifty dirham. The night of boozing has sapped my wallet. I find an ATM, but it tells me I have "insufficient funds". Rather than feel fear and freak out at this news, the magical time I have experienced gives me confidence that things will be okay. I note this response in me, because it's curious to experience it in the surrounds of a city-scape, and my usual anger and frustration at life has not yet kicked back in.

At that moment, a thought pops into my head - I've done it again. I have not thanked Ouarzazate for my time there, nor said hello to Marrakech on arrival. Duly taking some time out to do so, there in the middle of the busy street, I do both. It doesn't seem the sort of place that anyone will notice me acting strangely while standing in the middle of the road, and I am right. No one notices me at all. Then a short walk to the next ATM produces the scratch, and I am flush again.

I notice there are more walls and fences around things on the north side of the High Atlas range, and it is like being in a different country with a sense of claiming land, and of ownership, that is more defined. No one speaks to me on the street, though a gentleman in the shared Petty Taxi had helped ensure that I arrived at the station and then helped me find the correct window for my train ticket. He knew I was in no great shape, not just for translating, but for functioning at all. I was a dribbling wreck. I thanked him for his help, and he smiled knowingly at me and then continued on his way. People in the street don't stare, nor do they try to enter my space. I'm not sure if I miss that or not, but the mood has changed now. This being a city, I am just another person, anonymous again. Despite feeling cosmopolitan and adventurous from my travels, I am invisible, and it also feels like I am headed back into the belly of the machine. I can see signs of it here.

Travelling Through Time

Leaving Marrakech on a train bound for Casablanca, with nothing but grassland in all directions. I have a window seat in a four-seater cabin aboard a thundering diesel beast. Every seat is taken and the train appears to be fully booked, but it's comfortable and roomy enough. Out of the window I see farms, dirt roads, and the occasional building, that is mostly of adobe style shoe-boxes rather than homes of modern design. They are hand-built and fit well into their surroundings. It gives the scene a dated feel that is, to my eye, natural and appealing. The skies are clear and cloudless, though I wonder with all the green how often they stay that way. I am glad that I made this journey back by land and not by air, so I get to see it and gauge just how different it is compared to the southern deserts. I wonder if I will ever come back again. The moment I think this, a sadness overwhelms me. I already feel a nostalgic sense of attachment to this place that I have only so briefly spent time in, but I have lived each moment with such an intensity that I am dizzy from it. A sigh escapes me, an ache arising at the thought of having to return to my life back in London. What will I do when I get back there this time?

Feelings conjure as I watch the old and foreign world going by out the window. It's like a dream out of my reach that I am already forgetting, all the while aware that it is happening. Cross-country train journeys carry nostalgic sentiments. I have noticed it before and love them for it. Watching life going by out a train window as it rattles its way across a wild landscape in the fading afternoon sunlight. It's a unique delight, and I languish in it. As much as I am grateful to have experienced this trip, it also hurts to be letting it go. I wonder how I will feel when I get back tomorrow afternoon. Will all this seem real? Or will it have been nothing more than an interesting experience, and no longer feel like magical time? And now, watching the scenery pass by, it feels as if I am returning to the present from a trip into the past. Fate is more powerful in the old world, and everything functions there with a sense of connection to it. I was following the flow of that. Choosing from infinite doorways and opportunities as they passed by me. It's those moments that led me into the heart of a country from which I now have to return, and that transition is bitter-sweet.

The old man in the mountains keeps popping into my mind. There was something curious about him. The more I reflect on his being there, the more I wonder what it is that I am finding meaning in. Sometimes we cross paths with people that can affect us. We may not know it, but they can leave an indelible imprint upon us, sometimes even redirect the flow of our life. Elders, especially, can have this effect - they are the grandfathers and grandmothers of our time. The beings whom have seen the most, and certainly more than us, they are the *seers* and the *knowers*. No words need to be spoken, other than maybe a simple gesture of acknowledgement. He sat down opposite me after acknowledging me, not looking directly at me again, but just being there, which allowed me to observe him. New thoughts and ideas came to me as I studied his presence. There was something that I admired and respected about him, something I could sense, something he represented for me. He was calm yet powerful, and in that setting, I felt more aware of that. Often, in England, the old seem weak and a burden. Our culture has done this, taught us to dismiss the old. We no longer have time for them. To us, the old are not wizened beings, they cost money and are a hindrance. Bumbling around, we consider them an inconvenient annoyance that slows us down. They end up at odds with modernity, as it develops beyond their ability to function within its ever-changing parameters. They soon become the sum-total of their fears and concerns, and ours, too. We fear becoming like them. We hold a diminishing sense of value for their existence and often just wish them to be gone. What made us this way? Losing the value in our elders. It doesn't allow the old to be a strong reflection for us, nor to guide us. Instead, they get packed away in residential homes, their value lost, their minds drugged, and their experiences become isolated, valueless, and then forgotten. We prefer to forget about them, to avoid dealing with them, instead of taking the time to learn from their well-earned wisdom. Not having time to learn from the old means we have lost our way as a culture. We are left trying to appease the machines of modernity, as our life races ahead of us, and we run to catch up.

That old man in the mountains exuded a strength born of living in those mountains, there in the heart of nature, where time is allowed to slow down. The world around him so much older than mine, so much closer to the spirit than mine. Maybe he was a mountain tribal elder. He looked like one. Mine is a world of high speed and shallow concern. I try to imagine a life lived free of the machine, safe from it, up there in the mountains of Morocco where time might be permitted to stand still long enough to get to know a moment fully. What was I seeing in him as I watched him? Something had felt timely about his appearance in this story. And even now, thinking about him again with my eyes shut here in this carriage, I can feel into that moment. Something is there for me. He represented proof to me a proper way of living still exists out there somewhere, that the machine has not quite claimed us, that men and women still live beyond its reach in distant places. Places like that; in the mountains. My entire trip seems to have been about that same question. I am looking for something that is missing in my life. The Tuareg in the desert were longing for the world that I want to escape. I came out here looking for something that I felt certain I would find in this land. A clue, that if I could find it at all, I felt sure I would find it somewhere on the continent of Africa. I came out here to catch a taste of it, a hint in the air, maybe at its edges. Just to know if it is still here, or if it is gone now, lost to us forever. I don't know. I picture the old man in my mind, dressed in that dark green robe the colour of nature, and on his waist that curious ornate dagger with colourful gems mounted into the handle that I could not quite make out, but that looked like rubies and sapphires mounted in silver. It was a ceremonial knife, as symbolic as it was functional. The knife being a symbol of the hunter, of man's sharpened wisdom, and his ability to thrive alone in the wild. A knife is the most important tool a man can possess, along with a keen mind to wield it properly. It's symbolic of a man's grip on his own power. It told me he was in command of his senses. I tried to imagine our English retirees carrying ceremonial knives. Maybe they should. Then I remember that my grandad always carried a pocket knife on him. We don't forget our roots, not really.

I get up from my seat and go for a smoke out by the doors between the carriages. It's louder out there with the rattle of the train, but others are there with the same addiction and all we stand around quietly smoking. Lighting up, I suck in the addictive poisons and am gripped by anxiety and have a mild panic attack. It reminds me of how I function back at home in a constant state of fear and concern for the future. Thinking, planning, scheming to survive. There is no letup.

With each rattle of the tracks, I am returning to my normal state of being, and I do not look forward to getting back to that. I just cannot seem to beat the game, or rather am painfully aware that it is beating *me* now. Aware of the wear and tear that Time has taken upon me. I don't seem to possess the knowledge to protect myself from it any longer. In the city, life just swallows me up, and I have grown tired of the fight to beat the grind. I just keep losing ground as time passes by me and I get older and more tired. I guess sometimes we have to lose, and though I am not accustomed to it, there is a sense of inevitability in that. Maybe the old man represented immunity in some form, to that.

I wonder if I could survive in a place like the Atlas mountains. I want that cool certainty that I imagine the old man had. That sharp and keen knowledge to get by. Each moment lived calmly, purposefully, and at peace. What would I do there? If I took some time out to live my life as a nomad. Maybe travel its length, see what I found, and learn from whatever it could offer someone like me. Is that a realistic thing to want to do? I feel like a desperately lost soul looking for a path to follow. I need more soul-satisfaction in my life, but I am too afraid, too confused, and too jaded to know where to go or how to find it.

I also remain inexplicably addicted to the bright lights of the city, as if I owe it something that I can't yet give up. It has become my world. I don't want to give up my life in London, nor England, it's my home and always has been. But I can't stop for a minute, can't find rest in its constant demands and high cost of existence. I'm a hamster on a wheel, going round in endless circles. Now I have no home, I have become vagrant, floating, aimless, living in rentals that come and go, and living in a life that I feel unable to commit to. I am in limbo. Always moving on, but never finding a place to put my feet up, come to rest, and call my own.

London doesn't feel like home to me. It feels like a part of a long journey I have been on, always going somewhere else. But I have gotten so used to being there, that I don't know how to leave. Along the way, I've forgotten myself, forgotten what motivates me, and forgotten what purpose I had for being there in the first place. Dazzled, as I have been, by the big city glare. Yet at some point my values changed. I had this same thing happen when coming home from Spain the last time. I'd seen a solution while out there and hoped it might just fall into place by itself, but it never did. Instead, something came undone in me not long after that trip, and then I watched my life crumble down around me, like it was beyond my control to stop it from happening. I did nothing, just went along with it and let it fall apart. I didn't act to rescue the situation, because I knew I couldn't stop it. It was a strangely exquisite pain to be falling apart at the same time as I was being set free. But that freedom didn't feel like a healthy thing, more like a loss of everything that I had worked for. And when it was done, I just accepted the sense of failure that it left me with. And now the inevitable erosion of time has finally caught up with me. I disappeared for a while after that collapse, avoided people for a bit, and I don't think there was anything else I could have done. I'll write about that in another book on the time spent living in a van. But here I am now, coming alive again, and taking trips out once again. This time has been yet another pilgrimage looking for answers, but maybe I found some.

London always gave me the feeling that I was short on time, and I used to like that about it. It functions at a fast pace, and it requires energy to spin equally fast if you intend to stay afloat in it. I had that energy once, but no longer. When I first arrived there fifteen years ago, it drew me like a moth to the flame, and yet now it's the very thing about it that I struggle with the most. The time for me to leave London is not far away, but that means leaving all the people that I know. I would miss many people if I moved away. This last decade has brought me the best friends of my life. But it's my path and purpose now that is at stake if I don't act, and that's partly why I came out here; to do these crazy things and to see what revealed itself to me when I did. I *am* looking for something, maybe an answer, or maybe another way of life, or maybe it's just an idea. When I consider it from where I am right now, I realise just how alien life in London and the machine has become to me. I don't belong there any more. I am at a crossroads again, and this trip has shown me that it is time to act on that.

I put out my smoke and go back and find my seat in the carriage. We pass occasional tents, and I see goat herders on hillsides. Such simplicity of living compared to the complexity in the place that I live. Though the land must be owned here. Every available bit of it seems to have been cropped or tended and is in use. Out last night in

Ouarzazate, I realized Karim was illiterate, which was strange as he was so well educated about so many things, but I could tell it pained him for it to be discovered. I didn't see the problem, but I also understood how it is used to measure intelligence - or to imply a lack of it - and so it mistakenly defines a man's worth. This is something the machine has done to us.

Through the window, men plough fields with donkeys and horses, and others bend down as they hand-pick grasses. Our connection to the Earth, our direct connection to nature, and to our genuine sense of belonging and to home can be found through working with the dirt. While the intellectual functions from an aloof condition of self-reflection. Intellectuals live in a bubble looking outward, and obsessively analyse what we see, and this behaviour ultimately leads to insecurity and isolation. I know this because I have such a brain, and it drives me nuts. It's why I spent so long trying to drug it into oblivion. For me, intellectualism feels a lot like a lonely prison.

I see thin clouds. Long wisps hanging high in the sky. The goat herders create an odd melancholy as I watch them pass by. This train keeps travelling on through time. The connection to that old world diminishing the further on I go. Something tells me this simple way of life will ultimately be lost from the earth, and not just my nostalgia or lost to me. Something is making me want to cry in despair at this awareness I can not quite articulate. I could burst into uncontrollable tears right now, here in the carriage. I breathe to control my emotions and not let them escape or reveal themselves to my fellow passengers.

A young man sat opposite sprays himself with an overpowering and cheap chemical scent. He then puts shades on and looks pleased with himself. He did the ritual smugly, and it was not appealing. Is this what we have become? Just vain and shallow creatures obsessed with the reflection of ourselves.

Staadt goes by. It's a town with a more modern design and architecture that gives me the first sign of a return to modern habitation. It's changing now through the window of time, and I notice I am returning to a pleasant state of numb indifference right along with it. There is a relief in that, at least. I spy rubbish, abandoned machines, metalwork, piles of concrete, collapsed old buildings, signs of modernity and all its wasteful trappings.

We pull into a station and some passengers get off and others get on. Then we roll and move out again, leaving the town, headed on into more grasslands, then woodland, and then on through a thicker forest. More clouds build in the skies above, as we move forward in time and back to where I belong. Then, passing some red-tiled haciendas, a tall skyscraper comes into view. Casablanca, now just thirty minutes away.

Sitting opposite me is an old Moroccan lady. She is next to the young Moroccan man who smells of sickly chemicals that are still wafting through our carriage and linger at the back of my throat. Such contrast to one another, in their dress and their manner. He sits behind his shades almost offensively, while she seems to have a tear in her eye, and I wonder if she fears being here amongst us. She seems to be uncomfortable, as if this is her first time coming to the city. Maybe she is from the mountains. The cosmopolitan stench of egomania that is oozing from her neighbour is too much for me, so it must be a shock for her. It's hard dealing with all the unnatural horror of city life when you are not used to it. She kept smiling at me, as if she wanted me to help her out, maybe just to engage her. I couldn't fathom the sensation that I was feeling from her look, and I just smiled back and then continued to write into my notepad balanced on my lap. There is no way to help a single one of us. The train just rattles on taking us towards our destination. There is nothing any of us can do. And I no longer feel the need to try.

Ships That Pass In Moroccan Nights

Arriving in Casablanca as the sun departs the day. I head outside the station to discover that the air is much colder here. I stand for a while, taking it in. I've travelled a long way today, and it would make sense that the change in climate is noticeable. Large flocks of seagulls move over-head, their squawks telling me this is a port town. There is an obvious bustle and attitude here, and I'm again made aware that I am in a big city. There's a sense of vibrancy and again a feeling of anonymity in being here. I consider heading to the port, or maybe to find the beach-front, or to check out the centre for a while and wander around. I want to stretch my legs a bit. But after checking the map, I conclude I'm too far from any of these things and wonder if I can be bothered with it anyway, since tomorrow I'm going to be leaving early to get the flight out. It feels like the wind is out of my sails now, and I am not sure I have the energy to deal with city-folk. So instead, I take the easy option and book into the Hotel Ibis, which is conveniently located right next to the train station. It's time to relax and let the ever-growing sigh unfold within me and do its unstoppable thing. Don't fight it, just roll with it.

The hotel is expensive compared to the prices I was getting further south, but it's clean and hassle-free, which right now is exactly what I need. I can feel that inexplicable anxiety and ache, though it's likely the end of the hangover mixed in with the end-of-holiday blues. But I can't find pleasure while I am drowning in anxiety, which forces me into a place where I prefer to feel nothing at all. I want to be comfortably numb. I don't look forward to going home, but neither do I much dread it now. I am sleepwalking my way back in some kind of auto-pilot mode.

Going to my room, I take a shower to freshen up, then check out the TV channels and decide that a film can numb me later. I need numbing now, but I need a good meal first, so I head back down to the restaurant. It's open, but it's mostly empty. A melancholy music is playing quietly in the background. The lyrics are about going home. This is going to steer me towards more misery and wallowing, and decide I need to shake it off. I order a Heineken *to refresh the parts that other beers can't reach*, and then attempt to dispel the anxious mood by writing. After a while, I look up to catch a reflection of my unshaven self in the dark glass of a nearby sliding door. I look harsh, solemn, and serious.

I decide not to enter Casablanca looking for her charms tonight, but then wonder if maybe I should force myself to go out. But to do so might break this return phase that I have slipped into, and then just spin me off into dramas that I'm too tired to deal with. I'm at the last stage of this trip, and should relax into it. A part of me doesn't want to stay in the hotel, but I do so for all the right reasons, the sensible reasons. There has been adventure enough. I admit to feeling pensive at the prospect of going out, though I also fear the idea of staying in and missing out on something. It never goes away, does it? No matter how old and learned we become. Fear of people, fear of the unknown, fear of this and fear of that, it eventually becomes the fear of fear itself that makes our decisions. The fear of imagined dangers that lurk in the unknown. It's a practised fear. One day we will be correct about it, and it *will* get us. Maybe that is the problem.

To succeed in life, we must pretend we are brave enough, and strong enough, to achieve the thing we want to achieve, and even the bravest of them have to fake it at some point. *Fake it, to make it* - that is how natural-born losers can learn to become fearless warriors. To live a little can take large amounts of daring to achieve. The trick is to make like it was easy, while inside you might have been shivering like a child. You wouldn't believe how I felt before this trip. I was terrified, convinced it was going to be the end of me. To dare to push my boundaries and limits is difficult, and yet I do it all the same. For me, the idea of stagnating is much more terrifying. I prefer the freedom of travelling alone, but it hits me hard sometimes, despite my gift for leaping into the fray.

The other method I employ to escape the numbness of life is booze and drugs, though I am attempting to change that. Occasionally something unexpected comes along to break the routine, and then life seems fresh and exhilarating again, but the natural arrival of it is rare. Life really is quite dull. I think I would sooner die of terror than sit around waiting to die of boredom, and that is the only explanation I can give for my behaviour and my ability to take trips like these.

As for tonight, I simply have no energy left for going out. I have to sell this to myself, and I tell myself that it's the right thing to do, to just stay still and relax. I never could decide which is better: the excitement of going out - that is just frivolous and meaningless - or the comfort of the sofa and a woman to fall in love with. Though that often fades in its own way. Neither seems to be much better than the other, in the end. It's more a case of which one you prefer to indulge in at the time. Do that one.

I consider the anxiety that is still effecting me. Sex has been the number one best cure for it. Like a medicine, it works every time, at least for a while. I try not to go near drugs to resolve it, not medicinal ones, I mean. Recreational drugs served me well until the last few years. But sex cures my emotional maladies better than all the rest. Now I think about it, what I like about sex is probably more to do with the connection. And now my mind wanders to Casa's red-light district, but I quickly nip that idea in the bud.

Singing along quietly to the more up-tempo tune that is playing in the restaurant, I catch myself staring blankly at the other two loners that are now eating here. I wonder what their story is. I could ask, but I won't.

It's too soon to think about all that has transpired here. I am still in the middle of it and find it almost painful to look back at the last six days in my notes. So I look forward instead. Find something to entertain me and fire my synapses.

After some more mentally indecisive *to-ing* and *fro-ing*, I conclude I *will* hole up in my room and not waste any more of what little energy I have left dealing with the night-life of Morocco. I am about to head upstairs when I find a piece of a folded cigarette packet in my pocket. I unravel it to discover the word *"Uedas"* written on it. That is the name of the woman from Bar Obelix, and her phone number is written there too. I must have transposed it from my arm while in the club, though I don't remember doing so. I transfer it to my notebook, but I know I won't call her.

She was out of my league, and rather than that thrill me, I felt terrified by the thought. I consider calling her when I get back to England, even just to pass on my apologies to Karim for running off as I had. I'd promised to get his card from the shop before leaving town, but in my moody and drunken state had failed to even think about it. Leaving had been a rush, anyway. But these holiday connections come and go, and when I consider just how many ships have passed through my nights, I know I won't ever speak to Uedas or Karim again. Who am I kidding? I tried to re-connect with people I met on holiday once, and it was an awkward disaster.

I head up to my room. The show *"Medium"* comes on TV, with Patricia Arquette, and I stare lazily at it, not following the French audio-dubbing at all.

I soon fall asleep, and the television turns itself off by a timer that I had set, but a hard and rapid knocking on my door wakes me at midnight. I stumble through the darkness, find the light switch, and turn it on. Blinding myself, I immediately swear loudly and turn it off again, then fumble my way down the short corridor to the front door with coloured patterns now dancing in my eyes.

I can hear a noise outside the door, and people insisting I let them in. They are speaking English, but not natively. I have no intention of letting them in. Instead, I call through the door asking what they want. They seem sheepish, asking me to open it, but not explaining why. I don't trust them.

I stumble back to bed, get in, and then call reception to ask why I am being disturbed. They claim to know nothing of it. I insist they send someone up to deal with the problem. They call me back some-time later to tell me they don't know who it was. I thank them all the same, not wishing to be rude this time. It's not their fault, but it's peculiar.

Then I hear raised voices outside the door again. Someone is shouting. I stay in bed, no longer considering it to be my problem unless they take an axe to the door. No further knocks are forthcoming and it eventually dies down. The silence is followed a short time later by a call back from reception to tell me it was maybe another guest that had knocked, thinking it was their room. They apologise for the disturbance, and I thank them for dealing with it, then put the phone down.

I am wide awake now, and I lay in the dark staring up at the thin ambient light on the ceiling. Under my hands, I can feel the unique texture of starched hotel sheets. Hotel rooms always make me think of the women that have gone from my life. Mostly it reminds me of holidays spent with them in sunny climes. The feel of their tanned skin after days on the beach could bring a tired relationship back to life. There have been several good times spent with women in rooms, just like this one. When my mind is done wandering over the past, I start to wonder who will be in my future. Thoughts turn to *her* again - *the one that got away*. Uedas reminded me of her a bit. That same sense of being in a different class from me. Maybe that's what attracted me to her, and what made me feel unworthy. Even if I had been sober, I still wouldn't have had the guts to call her, and it was not because I was afraid of failing, but because I was afraid of starting something that I couldn't live up to, or finish.

The *one-that-got-away* theme seems to have popped up more than just a few times on this trip, and I wonder if I will ever settle down, or rather, if I will ever want to. I never have yet. Just sometimes familiarity happens, caused by time and the happy accident of not leaving them when maybe I should have done. When thinking these kinds of thoughts, and remembering the women who have been in my life, I find it's best to conjure up the best-of-the-best to warm the heart. Maybe that is what she does for me, the one that got away. She warms my heart with an unattainable, idealistic, feminine perfection. I am sure the ultimate partner is the one you never get to be with, because then nothing can go wrong and ruin it. They are the ones I think about on these lonely and sleepless nights, when I find myself awake in distant and solitary hotel rooms and a certain loneliness descends. Halfway across the planet and with no idea where I am headed at all, it helps to dream of a goddess, something beautiful to keep my heart and soul from growing cold. And the thought of her provides solace through these lonely small hours, when feeling somewhat abandoned by the universe, and the bats of anxiety are swooping in. I'm feeling a little sorry for myself, a little forgotten and discarded, and with a question of whether it is too late for me to change. Could I become a better man? Do I have to?

Uedas was younger than me, but her words echo around in my mind and it makes me feel good.

"I want to see you again," she'd said, and I think she even meant it, and I am pretty certain she wasn't a prostitute.

It was new to get such forthright honesty from a woman. English women are more reserved and want you to do all the work. It felt like Uedas had an immediate awareness that we could be a something. There was unmistakable clarity in how she spoke to me. She'd already decided exactly where it might get to, and how we might end up, probably years from now. It's the nature of women to do that. I'd been weighed, measured, and found *not* wanting, or so she thought. I wonder what her criteria had been? Whatever it was, I met it, and I guess that had surprised me. I don't see myself as a catch; I am an awful choice for most women for a bunch of reasons, and I know it. And I am pretty certain it wasn't my dance moves. Her interest complimented me, but I also knew that it would not have taken me long to ruin it. Whatever she thought she was seeing, she was wrong. I would have let her down in the end, and maybe that was why I would conveniently forget to call her. I, too, knew something was there between us, something that could have been beautiful. But I also know that I could never have sustained it. It scares me to even try. So, I had to let her down. Not calling her was the only right thing to do.

How odd it is that from such brief meetings and momentary dalliances that entire lives can become entwined and new life spring forth. History gets made in a split-second decision. We say hi to someone on the dance floor and the next thing we know we are married with kids. Many such actions and choices are indelible once we fall into them. The history of the world sits in our hands, or more accurately, the power is in other body parts that we have far less control over. Nature controls them, not us. What an absolutely terrifying thought. To be controlled by a crazy, serial-killer such as Nature. Decisions are such powerful things, and if we don't learn to make them, then something else will make them for us, and then we'll wonder what the hell happened to our lives and how it came to this.

The High Adventures Of The Unknown

I awoke from an exquisite dream. It had begun with confusion about my ex-girlfriend, when I discovered she had been having an affair with a gay male-friend for the two years before we split up. This was not true in real life. I was angry at her in the dream, not for the infidelity itself, but for the length of time it had been going on. I demanded an explanation, and was expressing my disgust when a man went by in the street and asked if she wanted him to call for help.

"Yes, I do want you to call for help!" I said to him, feeling unfairly characterised by his presumption.

The dream then changed, and I was forming a list: *"The things that warm my heart and soul"*. Each item held such deep pleasure that I became intoxicated with joy the more I worked on it. Some of those items I wouldn't know how to explain, they just had about them the very essence of magic and heart-warming certainty, as if they tapped into the source of happiness itself.

When I awoke, the feeling lingered, though it wasn't long before the real-world broke in and the sensation dissipated. But before it was lost, I recalled that there was a time when I had not been dogged by a constant anxiety. This anxiety has been going on for so long that I don't even notice it there half the time, and I've become so used to it being in my life that I can ignore it and function, regardless. The dream reminded me of a time when it didn't exist at all, of a version of myself that I have long since forgotten. There had once been an innocent and unadulterated joy that came with being alive, and I wondered what changed that.

I packed up my stuff and left the hotel, and the train was waiting at the station when I arrived. It gave me the odd sensation that it had been there waiting for me the whole time. I guess I was feeling emotional to be leaving. So much of the journey felt timely and had flowed. And I had followed it all with such an ease, that it surprised me how well it had gone. Maybe I was learning something, at last. I'd become a traveller in my attempts to re-discover this skill, and more than that, an adventurer.

The good, the bad, the beautiful, and the ugly. It's all out there to be witnessed, and while we have time, maybe we should try to witness some of it. Why else are we here? It's not just to collect possessions that we then leave behind for someone else to enjoy. And it all begs a question: does something guide our path through this mysterious world of space, time, and matter?

I came on this journey to fathom that out. God, Allah, Fate, Luck, the Spirit, call it what you will, but something is out there that can guide us through the dark and the unknown like a compass. This has not just been a vacation for me, but a pilgrimage, to connect with that once again, whatever *that* is. It's a forgotten way. At least that's how it feels, and it needs to be remembered through action. And all that it takes to flow with it, is a trust.

Ever since coming back from the Spain trip, I have been working on letting go of the mindset that has held me back from remembering how to connect to it. Little by little, something has shifted, and it's required a patient and gentle undoing to achieve. If it had been too sudden, I think I might have broken myself. Some moments have been painful, and sacrifices always have to be made. I think that is what makes it hard for most of us, to have to take that kind of responsibility is not easy.

I didn't come out here to take photographs, or to sight-see, or to sun myself on a beach. Nor did I come out here to buy a piece of land, or to take something back to hang on my wall as a reminder. Nor to have tales of derring-do to recount at fabulous dinner parties upon my return. I didn't even come out here to write a journal about my adventures, though I have. I came out here to test my ability to flow with life and remember how to fall into opportunity. I was wanting to feel alive again, and to throw myself into the high adventures of the unknown. To feel the power and magic of going with the flow, and to recall what that meant, while feeling the freedom to travel in any direction on a whim. I wanted to feel how something connects me to the world when I let go to that. I could see how each moment unfolded in such a way that it could take me anywhere if I let it. How would that then shape my life if I could live in this way all the time? If it could develop in me until it became something that I did every day of my life naturally.

This is what we have forgotten under the crush of the machine. Just by being removed from the machine for this short time was enough to know that the ability is still there within us, however dormant it might have become. It's in all of us still. All we have to do is let go and trust. Fall face-first into our fears, regardless of the consequences. Leap into the void. Sure, I might have died, I nearly did, but isn't that the essence of living? I could not have wished for a better journey or outcome, and going into the heart of Morocco was the perfect choice for me, I can see that now.

I board the train, find my seat, throw the rucksack on the one in front, and settle in. Soon after, a horn sounds towards the front. It sounds like a trumpet calling the hunt. A shiver goes down my spine and a burst of adrenalin goes through my veins. The chase, the race, is on. I am the hunter *and* the hunted.

The train strains and moves, gradually picking up a pace until we pass out of the station and are rolling on through the city of Casablanca. I wonder if I will ever come back to Morocco. If I do, it will be for the mountains and the magic I felt humming there. I want to know the mystery, the beauty, the divinity of all things. It would be easy to return, but then one can never tell what comes next. And isn't that the beauty of it, that freedom has a price and that price is sacrifice. I wonder what adventures await me, and where they will lead me, now that I know. I wonder if I will soon leave London, but it is almost inevitable that I must. There isn't much left to keep me there.

The train journey doesn't take long, and I alight at Mohammed International V airport terminal which is at the end of the line. I am not in a rush, and so I stand for a while as the platform empties of people and I smoke a last cigarette. Turning to watch the train reverse back out of the station, I watch it disappearing into the bright light of the exit at the end. I crouch down, putting the fingers of one hand against the smooth surface of the floor for balance. A loudspeaker plays a soulful lament, and the feeling captures me. I shut my eyes. Transfixed by its bitter-sweet longing, I let myself drown in it. It is so strong I want to cry. Tears that I sense exist somewhere beneath the surface, and that I never release to the light of day any more, are the last of my unbroken innocence. A dreamy state engulfs me, and I open my eyes to watch the last carriage of the train pulling out. The spirit of my trip is leaving along with it, and I voice my thanks and goodbyes as it recedes. The spirit that Morocco had lent me for a while is now leaving with that train. I linger in the echo of it for as long as I can keep it there, until the train has gone, and the sensation gone along with it.

Then I finish my smoke, stand up, and turn and walk towards the airport entrance. The noise and the chatter of the crowd within making it like I am walking into the surf of a vast ocean. I wonder about when Africa first came to collect me, but I know it was on that first night, as I was seeing the sky above Ouarzazate as we came in to land, and those two stars that had looked down on me, the eyes of the rattlesnake, my snake god, gently changing until they became a gateway to Africa. She'd invited me to enter, and all I'd had to do was follow her in.

*

her books by Mark DK Berry

The Road To El Palmar (Travel journal)

Rock Star (Fiction/Humour)
Pussy Productions (Fiction/Humour)

Broke (Poetry)
Leaving Town (Poetry)

For the latest publications visit www.MarkDKBerry.com